Healing LIVES

True Stories of Encouragement and
Achievement in the Midst of Sickness!

TOBE MOMAH

WESTBOW°
PRESS
A DIVISION OF THOMAS NELSON
& ZONDERVAN

Foreword by Pastor Shane Warren

Scripture taken from the King James Version of the Bible.

WestBow Press books may be ordered through booksellers or by contacting:

WestBow Press
A Division of Thomas Nelson & Zondervan
1663 Liberty Drive
Bloomington, IN 47403
www.westbowpress.com
1 (866) 928-1240

ISBN: 978-1-4908-3159-6 (sc)
ISBN: 978-1-4908-3158-9 (hc)
ISBN: 978-1-4908-3160-2 (e)

Printed in the United States of America.

Library of Congress Control Number: 2014905462

WestBow Press rev. date: 03/24/2014

I dedicate this book to Gbolahon Sokoya MD (1971-2012). He is chronicled herein as one of the Healing Lives and remains an inspiration for the writing of this book by his giving in life and graciousness in death.

Contents

Part IV: Healing Lives—Personnel

Part V: Healing Lives—Pastors

Foreword

Dr. Tobe Momah is a man of strong faith who not only believes in miracles but also walks in them. As a medical doctor, he brings a unique perspective on the topics of divine healing and the working of miracles. In this powerful book, he enumerates spectacular demonstrations of God's miraculous power. Reading this book will increase your faith and inspire you to believe God for greater things.

Pastor Shane Warren
The Assembly West Monroe

Acknowledgments

God inspired this book. He pointed me to people with stories of encouragement, accomplishment, and achievement, and He allowed me to put their words in print. This book, however, would not have been possible without other invaluable help I received along the journey from others who saw value in it and spurred me on.

More than anyone else, though, my wife of eleven years, Rita, provided a setting that encouraged me and sharpened my desire to write. She motivated and mentored me on several of the topics treated here, especially when it concerned females. It would have been a near-impossible task to finish this book without her invaluable support.

My church, the Assembly West Monroe, Louisiana, and my pastor, Shane Warren, inspired me to keep writing with their heartfelt worship, exceptional warmth and care, and the trailblazing Word. These enabling surroundings helped the dream of this book become a reality.

I also thank Andy and Janice Varino's Sunday school class, where I shared much of the material of this book, for their rapt attention and bold encouragement.

My parents, Dr. and Mrs. Momah, continue to inspire me with their unconditional love and steadfast loyalty to family. They have supported my outlandish projects again and again and can be relied upon for untiring camaraderie whenever I need it. My brothers and sisters—Amaka, Ada, Emeka, and Nkem—and their families were all instrumental in this book's completion, and I cannot overemphasize the importance of their help.

A member of my church and a retired English teacher, Mrs. Burke, proofread this book and gave me invaluable insight into the use of proper English lexicon and grammar. This book is a product of her painstaking editing work, and, even at age eighty-seven, she remains an inspiration of healing and faith for me.

Thanks also out to my publishers—Westbow Press—for their excellent staff and people-management skills. They were invaluable and second to none throughout the project.

Finally, I thank the supporters of my ministry, Faith and Power Ministries, for their ardent support and unflinching loyalty. They spurred the publishing of this book with their fervent enthusiasm and spirit when I shared portions of it at our monthly Holy Ghost Night meetings or in correspondence. May what you have made happen in my life be replenished multiple times in yours, in Jesus' name, amen.

Tobe Momah, MD, FAAFP

Introduction

God gave me the vision for this book in June 2012 at one of our Holy Ghost Night events in Monroe, Louisiana. He told me in a gentle whisper to "bind up the testimony; seal the law among my disciples" (Isaiah 8:16). His purpose in the chronicling of these testimonies was to extol God's supernatural works in the world today.

God emphasized that I should publish eyewitness accounts of healings I personally witnessed or verified. He did not want hearsay or told-me-so stories. It is similar to Elder John's testimony in 1 John 1:1: "What I... have heard [and] seen with my eyes [and] I have looked upon and my hands have handled of the Word of life."

This book was spurred on by the story shared on that Holy Ghost Night, and from then on, God gave me another ninety-nine cases witnessed directly or verified personally as evidence of the miraculous. I followed due medical diligence and an invigorative investigative acumen, and in every one of these cases, the supernatural hand of God was evident.

There may not always have been a physical healing or a spiritual deliverance, but in every case chronicled here, there was a miracle! A miracle is defined by the Free Online Dictionary as "an occurrence that is inexplicable by laws of nature and so is held to be supernatural in origin or an act of God."

Every one of these cases met that criterion. Each incident was inexplicable and divinely orchestrated by the supernatural God. My prayer is that as you read these stories of healing lives, you will experience your own miracle and add your name to this roll of heavenly witnesses of the miraculous working power of God. Happy reading.

Tobe Momah MD, FAAFP
West Monroe, Louisiana
October 2013

PART I

Healing Lives—Personal

You cannot invalidate what God values.

Chapter One

From Invalid to Invaluable

*Beloved, now are we the sons of God, and it doth not yet appear what we
shall be: but we know that, when he shall appear, we shall be like him*
—1 John 3:2

I was born the third son of a military professional and an astute
teacher. In my teens, I started having weekly asthma attacks that
were debilitating and deleterious.

Asthma, unfortunately, had a history in my family; my mother's
only sister had died from it in her thirties, and my parents were
determined I would not suffer the same fate.

I was ferried back and forth from hospitals to clinics. At a time,
my mother even considered taking me to a herbalist or traditional
medicine man in an attempt to fully restore my health.

Thankfully, sanity prevailed; she did not take me to these men! I
was kept away from typical childhood sports and chores. I carried an
inhaler with me everywhere.

He's an Invalid!

As with most other high schoolers, I engaged in sports and other
strenuous exercises. I was on the school cricket team and the house
soccer team and actively participated in sports against my doctor's
advice.

On one of those eventful occasions, I became ill and was rushed to the hospital with an asthma exacerbation. My parents had to come and pick me up from the high school boarding house, where I resided, and take me home.

As I was entering the house, I heard my father speaking in low tones to my mother. I strained to hear what he said, and what I heard jolted me. He said, "Tobe is an invalid and should desist from playing sports entirely."

I behaved as if I had not heard my father's words and went up to my room and wept. I considered an invalid to be someone who was a liability with little or nothing to contribute, and I knew I was invaluable, not invalid.

Even though I knew my parents loved me and meant no harm, the thought of abject abandonment of my dreams and aspirations at the feet of asthma built a spirited revulsion in me. I therefore determined to change the status quo!

Tobe or Not Tobe—That Is the Question!

God exalted me through high school and medical school and gave me a *primus inter pares* position among my family, faculty, and friends.

As soon as I surrendered my life to Jesus in 1989, the asthma condition that had beleaguered me for so long disappeared. My recurrent wheezing stopped, and I had no need for inhalers. My formerly invalid position soon became an invaluable one as my siblings and parents relied on me to ensure things were completed in the family.

God raised me up as a storehouse and distribution center for solving problems spiritually, emotionally, financially, and even physically.

My story was turned from invalid to invaluable by the power of God. Today, I stand as a testimony of what God can do in a life surrendered to Him.

Life lesson 1: When God starts, no one can stop Him!

What men call opposition, God calls opportunity; and what others see as a stumbling block, God sees as a stepping-stone.

Chapter Two

I Saw Hell

They that see thee shall narrowly look upon thee, and consider thee,
saying, Is this the man that made the earth to tremble, that did shake
kingdoms; That made the world as a wilderness, and destroyed the
cities thereof; that opened not the house of his prisoners?
—Isaiah 14:16–17

My brother Nkem had lived a riotous life. Moving from one party to the other and from one woman to the other, he was the life of any party he attended. Widely popular, a medical doctor, and with a respectable pedigree, he was in every way an eligible bachelor.

He had just taken our older brother to the airport when everything changed in his life. On his way back from the airport, he fell asleep at the wheel, ran off the road, and rolled his car over several times. As a result, he went into a state of unconsciousness for about twenty-eight days.

While Nkem was unconscious, I was in Enugu, Nigeria, praying for his quick recovery. I did not know from a medical standpoint the extent of his injuries, but God gave me assurance of his healing and deliverance. When he miraculously woke up twenty-eight days later, even the doctors were stunned.

It was even more amazing that he had no physical deformities or mental lapses. Anybody who saw the car wondered how he could have survived the crash, as his car was completely mangled. He remembered everything before the accident but nothing after it.

Hellish Coma

One thing he remembered, though, was visiting hell while he was unconscious. He woke up with a sense of foreboding. As a result, he decided to "clean up his act" and live for Jesus. He refused to engage in illicit sex with his girlfriend after the accident. To which she replied "Have you been talking to Tobe [the author]?"

God demonstrated His power to me through my brother's recovery. Even though he was not living for Christ at the time, the prayers of the saints on his behalf prevailed and pulled him out of the pits of hell.

Nkem is now using this singular event that transformed his life to point people toward Christ. He is now leading a large nonprofit that educates drivers about safe driving. God is the God of the turnaround breakthrough.

Life lesson 2: What God kills, no man can keep alive, and what God brings to life, no man can kill!

What you believe is who you become, and who you become is why you were born!

Chapter Three

The Day Physicians Thought My Father Would Die

God, who quickeneth the dead, and calleth those
things which be not as though they were.
—Romans 4:17b

y father had gone from Abuja, Nigeria, to Lagos, Nigeria, for a routine medical checkup. He had complained about an incessant cough associated with shortness of breath and wanted his cardiologist physician's opinion.

On arrival, the physician connected him to an intravenous diuretic, which threw him into a deranged electrolyte state. He became confused as bicarbonate (an organic acid) accumulated in his brain. He could not breathe independently as a result of the confusion, and the doctors at the hospital intubated him and placed him on a mechanical ventilator.

When news of my dad's condition reached me in the United States, I became perturbed and perplexed. I had spoken to my dad the night before his trip to Lagos. I could not understand how he had deteriorated so quickly. In my despair I cried unto God, and He gave me six steps to take that would change my father's situation permanently:

1. **Paid:** God told me He had paid for my dad's healing! He didn't need any additional sacrifice or payment. Jesus finished the

work of redemption at Calvary (John 19:30). No additional effort is necessary.

2. **Pray:** God told me to open my mouth and pray what I desired. He told me the words of my prayers were not mere words but mountain movers when asked in faith (Mark 9:23–24).

3. **Play:** God told me to relax! He cautioned me against carrying cares instead of "casting all my cares upon Him" (1 Peter 5:7). He asked me to cast off anxiety, pensiveness, and the tension-laden life my siblings and I were living at the time and rest assured in Him.

4. **Principles:** God reminded me to stick to the unshakeable principles of the Word of God. He warned me to let the Word reign in my life because "the scriptures cannot be broken" (John 10:35).

5. **Portray:** God asked me to portray what I desired. *Portray* means to "play the role of" (*Webster's English Dictionary*), and those who portray well become the picture they portray. He asked me to act as though what I desired were already present because that is how God acts (Romans 4:17).

6. **Prostrate:** Last, God told me to prostrate in worship before Him. He reminded me that when everything else fails, praise and worship never fail! It is what we were made for (Revelation 4:11) and what we will do for ever.

Nothing Wrong with These Lungs!

I took God's six-step counsel and stopped walking in fear and speaking unbelief. I told my siblings that even though my dad was still intubated and on a mechanical ventilator, to plan for his hospital discharge.

I spoke in faith and expectation, and everything turned around! Within twenty-four hours, my dad was extubated. After seventy-two hours, he was home.

Post discharge, my dad got to London for a follow-up. The lung specialist in London, who had collaborated with the specialists in Nigeria, on seeing my dad and reviewing his films, looked disappointed. He wondered aloud why the Nigerian specialists had displayed such forlorn hopes about my dad's respiratory condition when, going by what he could see, there was no cause for alarm.

My dad has since that time continued to live in health albeit with regular follow-ups with the specialists in London.

His near-death experience was a lesson for me in God I will never forget. Those six steps—paid, pray, play, principles, portrayal, and prostrate—have been etched on my heart and will forever be part of my Christian walk.

Life lesson 3: It is not over till God says it is over.

Where man ends is
where God starts.

Chapter Four

Crossover Champion

He [God] would grant unto us, that we being delivered out of the
hand of our enemies might serve him without fear in holiness
and righteousness before him, all the days of our life.
—Luke 1:74–75

My sister, Ada Momah, was a stellar junior student at the University in Minna in Nigeria, studying computer science, but she would suddenly have panic attacks and be bedeviled with fear, shame, and thoughts of doom.

Her course work was affected; after multiple visits to medical professionals, she had to abandon school to care of herself. Because of the dearth of professional care for her in Nigeria, my wife and I invited her to London to live with us and continue her care and education.

We took her to various clinical and social appointments, expecting a miracle at the hands of these highly sought-after professionals plying their art on Harley Street in London.

Unfortunately, she was none the better. For the second time, she had to drop out of university. Medicine had come to the end of its rope, and only God's deliverance could conquer this extreme fear and paranoia Ada suffered.

Crossover Night Miracle

I was at the 2003 Crossover service of my church in London, the Kingsway International Christian Center. At the service, Pastor Matthew Ashimolowo asked us to pray for one miracle.

I requested a turnaround in Ada's health and a supernatural intervention in her life. I called on God with strong crying and petitioned Him for a miracle. After that prayer, I knew God had healed Ada.

In a few months, I had to travel out of London on a ministry assignment. Ada was left without family and, with the care of her caregivers and social workers, she took care of herself.

Today, Ada is in Nigeria. She does not have those panic attacks and extreme terror attacks anymore. She comfortably interacts with strangers without fear.

Our greatest open secret as a family is that what you tell Ada will never get lost because she is an encyclopedia that never forgets. Her mind has been turned from fearful to fact-full. Today, she stands as a bulwark of God's power to change situations by prayer!

Life lesson 4: When you resist, you will be rewarded.

Until you give life all it takes,
you cannot take all it gives.

Chapter Five

A Family Reunited by God

And he shall turn the heart of the fathers to the children, and the heart of the children to their fathers, lest I come and smite the earth with a curse.
—Malachi 4:6

My uncle, T. W. (not his real name), was estranged from his wife. He had such a poor relationship with her that he described the marriage as a struggle in which only one partner could survive.

While she lived abroad, he lived in Nigeria. She had forcibly taken the children and wanted them kept incommunicado from him.

Though a successful businessman, he had allowed his family to spiral out of control. He could no longer talk to his children, and the situation was further worsened by the sudden demise of their mother, his estranged wife, in America. He suddenly went from being the victim to being the villain. His children accused him of nefarious attacks on their mother that had resulted in her death even though she was more than ten thousand miles away.

T. W. asked for God's help. He realized he could do nothing to turn the hearts of his children toward him and humbly acceded to divine help.

We prayed together, and I quoted Malachi 4:6 to him. It is a promise of divine reversal of ill-fortune and of turning hardened hearts back to God. He believed and started rapprochement talks with his children.

Restored, Revived, and Renewed

It appeared at first as though T. W.'s prayers would never manifest. But one after the other, each of his children came to him and were reconciled with him. Today, T. W. has been restored to all his children and is in constant touch with them. The bitterness, strife, and anger they had has given way to love, unity, and tolerance of each other.

In his latter years, the house of T. W. is growing stronger. He has just welcomed his first grandchild and looks forward to divine benevolence for the next generation.

Life lesson 5: All the Word for all of God!

God gives experiences,
not experiments.

Chapter Six

Heaven's Hands on Human Hearts

Herein is our love made perfect, that we may have boldness in the day of judgment because as he is, so are we in this world.
—1 John 4:17

My mother, Mrs. Christy Momah, is an avid Bible student and fervent prayer warrior. She had suffered unusual chest pains for about a week and was repeatedly short of breath and easily fatigued. She, however, dismissed her symptoms as the result of osteoarthritis or bone pain.

Her orthopedic surgeon recommended a chest X-ray and thought nothing further about it, but the pain persisted and began waking her up at night. This was unlike osteoarthritis pain that typically showed up only after walking or other activities.

One fateful day, while climbing the stairs of a two-story building, she began feeling dizzy and was about to faint. She called my older brother, a family physician in the same city. He asked her to go to a nearby hospital for a computer tomography (CT) scan of the chest.

God's Hand Helps Hearts

My mother went to the hospital, where the radiologist diagnosed her as having a blood clot in her lungs, otherwise called pulmonary embolus. She had been walking around with certain death at her heart's door except for the hand of God that had kept the blood flowing from her lungs to her heart seamlessly.

Pulmonary embolus kills at least 150,000 people in the United States alone annually. It acts with suddenness and usually ends in tragedy. Most cases are misdiagnosed because the victims are considered "sudden death" patients and wrongly categorized as having had a heart attack.

My mother went on anticoagulants for a year and is now stabilized. Her repeat CT scans are clear, and she has no symptoms of chest pain or shortness of breath. Now healed, my mother epitomizes the undeniable mercy and protection of a loving God even when we were unaware of the problem.

A few months before this incident, I remember praying fervently for my mother. I had a dream about the diatribe of death monopolizing my mother's family, and when I told my mother my concerns about the spirit of death beleaguering her family, she waved it off as coincidence and misadventures in life.

Four of her siblings had died prematurely and suddenly, and on that fateful day, I took authority over the spirit of death in her genealogy. After her close encounter with death, however, she now sees those prayers as God's hand preventing untoward calamity to her and us, her family.

Life lesson 6: Whose report you believe will determine what results you receive.

PART II

Healing Lives—Places and Persons

Laughter is the only medicine without any side effects.

Chapter Seven

Forgiving, Forgetting, and Fruitful

A merry heart doeth good like a medicine: but a broken spirit drieth the bones.
—Proverbs 17:22

D. K. (not his real name) was playing soccer on the streets of Kaduna, Nigeria when his whole world fell apart. At the tender age of eleven, he was rendered an orphan by Islamic fanatics who killed his parents in cold blood for professing Jesus Christ.

D. K. was rescued by his uncle, and as the sole survivor of his parents, was ferried abroad for safety. The pain of losing his parents, his siblings, and every semblance of the home he had grown to know was unfathomable.

Rather than bemoan the situation and dwell in self-pity, he resolved to make his dead parents proud. He forgave all who had hurt him, put the past behind him, and focused on his future.

Fruitful 21

D. K. has been a meteorite of firsts since showcasing his soccer skills in the United Kingdom. From playing in the back parks of Crystal Palace, he has risen to the top of the premiership in less than ten years.

He has played at all levels of the junior national teams and is currently a regular at his club, considered one of the elites in English soccer, and his national team. He was recently voted most valuable player for the African champions, Nigeria, in the 2012 Cup of Nations Tournament.

At twenty-one, D. K. is unarguably a multimillionaire with even greater heights beckoning. In spite of all that happened to his family in Nigeria, D. K. has returned to Nigeria and was featured proudly in the national colors for its soccer games.

He refuses to live in the past and remains grateful for whatever he has. When asked the secret to his success and meteoric rise at the age of twenty-one, the soccer star says, "I have to thank God for being where I am. It is like a dream come true."

Life lesson 7: Give no place, no matter how small, to the Devil.

A seed does not leave your life. It goes into your future and multiplies.

Chapter Eight

Turkanaland: A Land God Healed

Who hath heard such a thing? who hath seen such things? Shall the earth be made to bring forth in one day? or shall a nation be born at once? for as soon as Zion travailed, she brought forth her children.
—Isaiah 66:8

The people of Turkanaland, Kenya, have borne the brunt of famine and deprivation for decades as a result of lack of water. Their part of Kenya had a 37 percent malnutrition rate with 9.5 million people affected by the 2011 drought.

The desert conditions prevalent in Turkanaland affect cattle, farming, and especially humans. The average Turkanaland native walks at least ten miles daily to obtain water for basic subsistence needs and so leaves this northwestern enclave of Kenya short of suitable manpower from schools and education.

In 2012, French scientists commissioned by UNESCO began seismic studies looking for underground water or mineral reserves. At the same time, a Kenyan couple working in Louisiana (Sammy and Mary Murimi) began praying for healing over Turkanaland. They prayed from 2 Chronicles 7:14.

If my people, which are called by my name, shall humble themselves, and pray, and seek my face, and turn from their

wicked ways; then will I hear from heaven, and will forgive
their sin, and will heal their land.

Alongside other American missionaries, Sammy and Mary went
on annual Short Term Outreach and Relief Missions (STORM), and in
2003, while praying for rain for Turkanaland's desert, God told them
they didn't need rain but water.

Like a Flood

The seismic studies uncovered five underground pools in
Turkanaland, and the largest was the size of Rhode Island and contains
about two hundred million cubic meters of fresh water.

This body of underground water is called an aquifer and it is
naturally replenished by rainfall at the rate of 1.2 million cubic meters
per year. It is 330 meters below the surface and projected to last at
least seventy years.

This discovery has single-handedly changed the economy of the
Turkanaland people. They now have borehole water access and, in no
time, the farmland that had been so marginal will become irrigated
and sustainable.

The healing of the Turkanaland has turned those who were in
the cold clutches of poverty into the most sought out landholders in
Kenya. The prayer of Sammy and Mary Murimi and other missionaries
for the healing of the land has come true, and Turkanaland will never
be the same again.

Life lesson 8: God gives birth to a nation in a day.

Your allocation in God depends on your location on earth.

Chapter Nine

Positioned For Prosperity

When a man shall take hold of his brother of the house of his father, saying,
Thou hast clothing, be thou our ruler, and let this ruin be under thy hand:
In that day shall he swear, saying, I will not be an healer; for in my house
is neither bread nor clothing: make me not a ruler of the people.
—Isaiah 3:6–7

T. J. (not his real name) returned to his local community after hurricane Katrina in 2005. As a successful lawyer in New Orleans, he had amassed wealth, fame, and fortune. When everything went under, however, he chose to return to his hometown of less than five thousand.

He built up a reputation as an astute and honest citizen and was soon on the city council as legal adviser. When Faith and Power Ministries commenced in his town in July 2010, he and his mother were the only people, other than my wife and me, to attend the inaugural Holy Ghost Night.

At that night vigil, I gave a prophecy by the Spirit of God that someone aged thirty-nine was being set up for a promotion in the not-too-distant future. Since he was within that age category, all eyes peered in his direction.

A Leader and a Healer

In 2011, T. J. was elected to the state House of Representatives by a landslide victory. He went to the state capitol to champion the cause of the helpless and to be a voice for the hopeless.

As a baby, T. J. had been reared by a single mother. His father had abandoned him and his mother at his birth and was not a part of their lives. As his mother's only child, he persevered and, against all odds, became valedictorian of his high school class.

He sees his mission in politics as a healing one. He, as Isaiah 3:6–7 clearly illustrates, considers politics not a profession but a vocation, a way to give back to the society that made him who he is.

Through his efforts in the capitol, millions of dollars for a nursing home, orphanage, and school improvements have been disbursed. His presence at that night vigil and his presence in his local town have turned T. J. from a heaper of resources to a healer of the land.

Life lesson 9: God has no favorites, just those who fear Him and follow His instructions.

Fear is emotional embargo on the supernatural.

Chapter Ten

Too Shocked to Speak

And were beyond measure astonished, saying, He hath done all things
well: he maketh both the deaf to hear, and the dumb to speak.
—Mark 7:37

R. T. (not her real name) had been looking forward to March when she expected to deliver triplets without complications. Her expectations, however, were not to be.

She had ruptured her amniotic membranes and went into premature labor. Seventy-two hours later, she had lost all three children in quick succession. She was in a state of shock and could not utter a word.

R. T.'s mother was a patient of mine and had intimated to me earlier of her soon-to-be-born triplets. When their deaths occurred, she told me and asked me to pray for her daughter's recovery.

When God Speaks, Nobody Can Silence You!

After the death of her triplets, R. T. did not speak a word for three months. She was in a state of grief, and her medical personnel placed her on a round-the-clock suicide watch. No amount of persuasion by her husband or immediate family would make her open her mouth. She was in a deep state of mourning as a result of her loss.

During that month's Holy Ghost Night, we raised up prayers, especially for R. T. In unison, we commanded the spirit of heaviness and depression weighing R. T. down to depart and for her to begin to speak again.

Within two weeks, R. T.'s mother came to the clinic and told me R. T. was speaking again. In fact, God had healed her heart to the extent that she and her husband were already making preparations to have another child.

Those who went to mourn with her over her loss were surprised to see her excited and ebullient again. The spirit of heaviness was cast out, and the oil of gladness manifested by the spirit of prayer!

Life lesson 10: If the Devil can steal your praise, he can stop your goods.

It is not hard living for Jesus;
it is hard living on the fence.

Chapter Eleven

A Girl Named Christian

The Lord is not slack concerning his promise, as some men count
slackness; but is longsuffering to us-ward, not willing that any
should perish, but that all should come to repentance.
—2 Peter 3:9

O n my usual Tuesday evening preaching circuit, I met a very interesting woman named Christian. She had been named Christian because her birth was nothing short of a miracle.

For about ten years, Christian's mother had struggled to have a baby. She had had six successive miscarriages and was at the end of her rope when a traveling evangelist, Jesse Duplantis, came to her town in the early 1980s.

According to Christian, who related this story to me, Evangelist Duplantis called out her mother and prophesied to her that she would have a child. He replayed her life course to her and told her the curse of miscarriage was broken and she would bring forth a child.

Nine months later, that baby was born. The mother named her Christian in gratitude to the Lord Jesus Christ for her life. Her birth was a miracle that stirred a realization of the almightiness of God and humanity's smallness to Christian's mom.

A Waste of a Life

Christian started mixing with the wrong crowd in high school. Soon after, she had two children by unknown dads. She struggled to feed them and was soon frequenting the club and drug scene, looking for the ever elusive dollar.

At the time I saw her, Christian had been married and divorced twice. She was unemployed and taking care of two children by herself. She lived in a run-down part of the city and was involved in prostitution and drugs.

After hearing the miraculous story of her birth and having preached the gospel to her, I left sad because instead of projecting the glorious gospel through her life, Christian was wasting her life on drugs, alcohol, and other social vices.

Six months later, I received a text from a mutual acquaintance stating that Christian had overdosed on drugs and had lapsed into a coma. She died soon after leaving her two children and her mother.

She was a healing life because her birth demonstrated God's omnipotence. Her death, however, demonstrated His ultimate judgment. Galatians 6:7 says, "Be not deceived; God is not mocked: for whatsoever a man soweth, that shall he also reap."

Life lesson 11: People who love God don't need miracles to obey. Those who don't, on the other hand, seek miracles first before they obey.

*Life becomes more inspiration
and less perspiration
when you know Christ.*

Chapter Twelve

A Child's Miracle Birth

By thee have I been holden up from the womb: thou art
he that took me out of my mother's bowels.
—Psalm 71:6

V. W. (not her real name) was a regular twelve-year-old student in her rural community. Her life was changed, however, when she was sexually assaulted by an older neighbor. After more than six months of covert sexual relationship with this older molester, she began to have unusual abdominal pains.

Not thinking much of it, she took over-the-counter medications such as acetaminophen and ibuprofen but with no amelioration of the pain. She knew instinctively that something was wrong and called the emergency medical team (EMT).

Thinking she was a regular twelve-year-old with stomach cramps, they arrived totally unprepared for what they saw.

God Help Me to Help Her!

The physician on call received an urgent call from the EMTs at about 11:00 p.m. asking him to come immediately to the girl's house. When asked why he had to be present, the EMT said, "I think you need to see this for yourself."

On arrival, he found a twelve-year-old girl with a footling breech (legs first) delivery in active contractions. The nearest obstetric hospital was at least an hour away, and an air evacuation would compromise the baby's life.

V. W.'s pelvis was underdeveloped to handle full-term breech deliveries, and there were no sophisticated equipment such as forceps or vacuum extractors. He noticed that the baby's leg was turning black and that she needed urgent intervention.

At this point, he prayed that God would help him help her. Miraculously, the baby, though in a breech position, was successfully delivered with no defect. The baby was airlifted to a neonatal intensive care unit. The baby is currently three years old and in excellent health.

V. W. is in middle school and has finally come to terms with the fact that she was eight months pregnant and unaware of it! Her family has been very supportive, however, especially with caring for V. W.'s child.

The villain who impregnated her has been arrested and sentenced for pedophile crimes. Her life is a healing life because it shows what God can do in spite of all our shortcomings.

Life lesson 12: Child birth is 99 percent divine inspiration and 1 percent human perspiration.

Get on fire for God and the world will come and watch you burn.

Chapter Thirteen

Third Day and the Suicidal Kid

The thief cometh not, but for to steal, and to kill, and to destroy: I am come that they might have life, and that they might have it more abundantly.
—John 10:10

N o life is an accident; every life is a divine investment for future greatness. God sent His son, Jesus, by the power of the Holy Spirit to "bring many sons unto glory by making the captain of their salvation perfect through sufferings" (Hebrews 2:10).

A young man in New Jersey thought otherwise. He was young, capricious, and wanted to end it all. He felt like a failure at life and thought the best way out was to drive into a forested area and kill himself.

He loaded his gun and drove as deep into the dense woods as he could. Before he shot himself, however, he wanted to listen one last time to his favorite radio program. Unfortunately, because of how far he was from modernity, he could not pick up any radio signals except a Christian radio station in New Jersey. It was playing a song, from Third Day's "Born Again" album. He had the gun loaded, and its cold muzzle was on his forehead as he listened to the words of the song.

Total Turnaround

As he heard the lyrics, he lowered his gun. He listened to the lyrics, which said God came to give us life and love we had never known before, and he started weeping.

He confessed his sins to Jesus and asked for forgiveness at that moment. He drove out of the forest and back home, fully restored. He gave his life to Jesus because he had heard a song proclaiming the healing love of Jesus' name.

At an amphitheater setting in New Jersey during one of Third Day's concerts, this young man came forward and shared his testimony. Mac Powell, the lead singer of Third Day, who had composed that song while doing his laundry, said, "This makes it all worth it."

This young man from New Jersey is a healing life because he overcame the death of the world to taste the life of God by the love of God.

Life lesson 13: One word of inspiration is worth a million of mere information.

Fame is a vapor, popularity is an accident, and riches take wind. Character alone will endure.

Chapter Fourteen

Mary Slessor—Savior of Twins

But the midwives feared God, and did not as the king of Egypt commanded them, but saved the men children alive... Therefore God dealt well with the midwives: and the people multiplied, and waxed very mighty.
—Exodus 1:17, 20

Mary Slessor was a Scottish missionary who spent forty years working in the hinterland of the Efik in Nigeria. She was grieved by the practice of murdering twins in Calabar, Nigeria, and set about rescuing them. She traversed the Efik and Ibo nations, canvassing for this cruel cultural belief to be dropped.

The culture of killing twins developed because the tribes thought that twins were a result of a curse caused by an evil spirit who fathered one of the children. Twinning was considered a "disease" in their primitive mentality, but the treatment—brutally murdering both twins—was worse!

Eventually, Mary Slessor rescued hundreds of babies from slaughter. She established schools and vocational institutes for these abandoned children and their shamed mothers to come to learn trades and professions.

The outcome of this was the establishment of Christianity as the predominant religion of the area and the advancement of Mary Slessor as a judge over the people and the queen's representative to south-south Nigeria.

She never married, but on her death in 1915, after forty years in the harsh hinterland of Calabar region, many adopted children she had single-handedly saved surrounded her.

A Modern-Day Heroine

Today, in Calabar, Mary Slessor is considered a modern-day heroine. Her burial place is a tourist attraction, and most notable monuments in the city bear her name or insignia.

Without prerequisite training or military might, she stopped a culture that had been entrenched among the people by the Devil. What she did reverberates with every twin birth celebration in Nigeria today.

She is a healing life because through her, several lives were delivered from certain death for now and for eternity. At her death, the British consul gave her a state burial and published her death in the government gazette.

Life lesson 14: We cannot all do great things but we can all do small things with great love. —Mother Teresa (1910–1997)

God answers prayers in more ways than we can humanly imagine.

Chapter Fifteen

The Gift That Made Others Green

He that goeth forth and weepeth, bearing precious seed, shall doubtless
come again with rejoicing, bringing his sheaves with him.
—Psalm 126:6

Mart Green is the Oklahoma-based billionaire and chief executive of MARDEL and Hobby Lobby group of companies. A born-again Christian, he has been in the forefront of fulfilling the gospel's message in film, media, and book format.

He has single-handedly sponsored crusades to the Third World, produced films from a Christian viewpoint, and supported causes that have made him a bundle of life for institutions such as Oral Roberts University (ORU).

The Beginning

ORU was founded by a vision God gave to Evangelist Oral Roberts in the 1960s. He said, "Raise up your students to hear My voice, to go where My light is dim, where My voice is heard small, and My healing power is not known, even to the utmost bounds of the earth. Their work will exceed yours, and in this I am well pleased."

The university was opened in 1965 with three hundred students and has since produced stellar Christian alumni in law, science,

45

politics, religion, media, and other fields. It has its own international cable television station and pioneered the whole-person concept of education.

The Blessing

In the midst of its resounding growth, ORU became beleaguered and burdened by debt. In its 2007–2008 operational year, it had a budget of $87 million and a debt burden of $52 million. Its medical/dental schools were closed in the 1980s, and its law library was relocated to Regent University, Virginia.

In 2007, a financial healing miracle took place in ORU. The Green family agreed to give $70 million to stave off the university's debt and an additional $40 million to improve infrastructure if the university's leadership was streamlined and global, best business practices introduced.

The board of ORU unanimously agreed, and a new leadership team, headed by Dr. Mark Rutland, was instituted. By 2009, ORU was debt-free, and new infrastructure, which included a student center and an international multimedia studio, were constructed.

The Birth of a New ORU

Chancellor Roberts passed away at age ninety-one in 2010. At the time of his death, this great healing evangelist, who had seen the blind see and the cripple walk, wanted one last healing miracle. That miracle was the healing of ORU.

Through the Green family and other benefactors, the healing has begun, and a new dispensation for ORU is been birthed. ORU has carved a niche in Christian education that is hard to emulate. It has become the Christian liberal arts university of choice for young Christians of all denominations because one man chose to be a healing life to the body of Christ that was in need.

Life lesson 15: There will be no shortage in heaven.

PART III

Healing Lives—Patients

> *Since Jesus is the way, you cannot get lost; since He is the truth, you can't be deceived, and since He is the life, the Devil cannot kill you.*

Chapter Sixteen

Man's Incidentaloma Versus God's Inerrancy

Who is he that saith, and it cometh to pass, when the Lord commandeth it not?
—Lamentations 3:37

R. C. (not his real name) had a routine medical visit in my office and left for work. On his way, he had a wreck involving another driver. Paramedics took him and the other victim to a nearby community hospital for evaluation.

In the emergency room, R. C. went through routine evaluations. He had a chest X-ray and routine labs, and because he felt okay, he didn't expect any negative outcomes.

He was wrong! The chest X-ray showed a 7.5 cm right lung mass that was eroding into the wall of the chest. There were no obvious metastatic lesions, and R. C. was immediately referred to a tertiary care center for an incidentaloma, a tumor found by coincidence or incidentally and without any symptoms or suspicion. But this one looked like lung cancer.

In the Volume of the Book

As a believer, however, R. C. subscribes to the inerrancy of Scriptures. He knew "All things work together for good to them that love God, to them who are the called according to his purpose"

(Romans 8:28) and that I "come in the volume of the book [as] it is written of me to do thy will" (Hebrews 10:7).

He had quit smoking years before this incident and had no relevant family history of cancer. He was in his early forties, and he believed the inerrant Word of God was working for his good.

He underwent radical excisional biopsy of the mass, which was confirmed as cancerous. The doctors told him that he did not need chemotherapy or radiation therapy because he had presented early enough to stave off metastases and the surgical operation had gotten all the cancer.

He returned to work and remains asymptomatic to date. He chides people not to think of life as an incident but as a well-planned and orchestrated divine setup for our lift up. He says what the Devil meant to kill him—a motor vehicle accident—God turned around for his good.

Life lesson 16: Whatever upset the Devil starts always ends as a setup for us by God if we follow God's script.

Until you learn to be silent before God, you will be silenced by men.

Chapter Seventeen

Restored, Revived, and Ready to Die

I have been young, and now am old; yet have I not seen the
righteous forsaken, nor his seed begging bread.
—Psalm 37:25

T. U. (not her real name) came to me asking for skin-cleansing cream. She was in her late forties and pretty; she had a small frame and was loquacious. I got her face cleansed with some topical medications, and on her return appointment, she was very appreciative, so appreciative that she consented to a routine blood test.

On her first visit, I had noticed her evasiveness to my running any lab tests. On her second visit, I was determined to run routine laboratory screens and that included a HIV (human immunodeficiency virus) screen.

The test returned as positive for HIV. T. U. returned for a follow-up appointment and when confronted with the result, she confessed to having held back some vital information initially.

She acknowledged having been diagnosed with HIV in 1990 while pregnant with her second child. She refused treatment at the time, fearing it would hurt her child.

She was diagnosed again with HIV in 1995 while incarcerated in the Louisiana State Penitentiary system. After staying there for less than a year, she was released without any antiretroviral treatment or medical follow-up.

Cleaned Up

T. U. came to a knowledge of Christ in prison, and she had surrendered her life to Jesus. She returned to the outside world stigmatized, ostracized, and pilloried for no good reason.

When she couldn't keep other jobs, she turned to cleaning churches as a profession. As she cleaned, God healed her.

While in a Sunday night service, T. U. saw the vision of a portrait of the healing Jesus with stripes on His back. The man of God prophesied to her that God would heal her irreversibly and that she would walk in divine health in spite of her circumstances.

Irreversibly Irrevocable Blessings

T. U. took that irreversible, irrevocable, and blessed Word and has run with it for nearly twenty-three years. She worked at a high-brow hotel as a housekeeper and supplements her income by offering catering services to the public.

She has continually refused to acknowledge the presence of HIV in her body even though her viral load is greater than two million copies.

She has worked for her and her children's upkeep as a single mother without any public assistance, health insurance, or other benefits accruable to someone with HIV. She says she would rather die and meet Jesus than acknowledge HIV and die an invalid victim of a chronic disease.

To T. U., acknowledging the presence of the disease is tantamount to rejecting the Word of the Lord spoken to her in 1995. She has stood on God's promises for nearly twenty-five years and has survived the twin menace of HIV and AIDS.

She has done all this without taking a single antiretroviral medication. Her children born during the time of her diagnosis with HIV are all healthy and have made T. U. a proud grandmother.

Life lesson 17: It is better to die in faith than to live in doubt.

What you compromise to keep, you will lose, and what you lose to compromise, you will keep.

Chapter Eighteen

Solution to Syphilis

There came also a multitude out of the cities round about unto
Jerusalem, bringing sick folks, and them which were vexed
with unclean spirits: and they were healed every one.
—Acts 5:16

G. M. (not her real name) was impetuous when I met her. She acted as though she had no reason to live. As a child, she had been abandoned by her father and raised by a single mother. When G. M. was in her late teens, her mother died suddenly from breast cancer. As a result, she became homeless and without any family. Her mother's family callously blamed her for her mother's early demise, and her father didn't want anything to do with her.

She had attempted suicide repeatedly, used habit-forming illicit drugs, was on mental-health medications, and was completely disillusioned when I met her. To add to her misery, laboratory tests revealed a new diagnosis of syphilis.

Repressing RPR

Syphilis is a sexually transmitted disease with widespread effects on the body if not treated. G. M. was still in her teens, and the aftereffects of the disease could permanently impair her cognition, fertility, and mobility.

I invited G. M. to church and took her to one of the Holy Ghost Night prayer meetings my wife and I were leading. Between these meetings, she gave her life to Christ at our local assembly and started a new lease of life as a Christian.

When as a matter of routine I rechecked her for syphilis, it had disappeared! She had not taken any medication during this three-month period because she had chosen to live in denial instead of confronting the disease. Subsequent rapid plasma regain (RPR) tests verified that she had been cured without treatment. G. M. was ecstatic, and she glorified God as a result.

She is currently disease-free, and my wife and I continue to encourage her to apply the same healing power in Jesus' name to her other emotional, physical, and spiritual wounds. The same God who was able to heal one malady can certainly heal all others!

Life lesson 18: God has no favorites, only those who fear Him and those who don't.

The Devil can't stand you, can't stop you, and as long as self is no more, there is nothing he can do against you.

Chapter Nineteen

Stage IV Cancer in Brooklyn

A merry heart doeth good like a medicine but a broken spirit drieth the bones.
—Proverbs 17:22

A. A. (not his real name) was a thirty-nine-year-old African-American male I admitted to the hospital in Brooklyn, New York. He had been healthy until a few days before his admission and presented with shortness of breath, easy fatigability, and chest pain.

He neither smoked nor drank and had a decent job with a Fortune 500 company in Manhattan. His test studies showed he had an impending pericardial tamponade, a condition with a large amount of fluid around the heart, and he had to undergo immediate surgical intervention to relieve the pressure.

He successfully underwent surgery, and the fluid evacuated was sent for study. The results came back a few days later showing stage IV metastatic cancer, most likely from the lungs.

As I walked into his room to break the news to him, I was apprehensive about how he would take it. I was, however, even more shocked at his response!

Cancer Can't Kill Me!

When I broke the devastating news to him, A. A. simply shrugged his shoulders and matter-of-factly asserted that cancer could not kill him. He said the fact that he had survived drug abuse, hooliganism, and gang membership on the streets of Brooklyn meant that he could outride this current storm.

Apparently, A. A. had been abandoned as a child to the backstreets of the "hood." He had had a derelict dad and a wayward mom, and he had single-handedly raised himself. He had risen through the ranks at his job by sheer determination and personal faith in God and was pursuing educational advancements at the time.

A. A. stood fearless in the face of what would have made others tremble because he knew in whom he believed. He was counseled to "Go home and die" by the specialists because of the aggressiveness and advanced stage of the cancer.

Three years later, however, A. A. was still at work and healthy without any direct medical intervention. His will to live and faith in God saw him through what would certainly have been a death knell for others.

His infectious optimism changed my approach to end-of-life and palliative-care patients. A positive attitude can overcome any tumor or turmoil as long as you let God's Word prevail!

Life lesson 19: Life is not a function of aptitude but of attitude toward God's Word.

*In the ridiculous instruction lies
God's miraculous intervention.*

Chapter Twenty

Second-Term Pregnancy without Striking Features

Notwithstanding she shall be saved in childbearing, if they
continue in faith and charity and holiness with sobriety.
—1 Timothy 2:15

R. S. (not her real name) was a morbidly obese twenty-eighty-year-old patient of mine who was in a stable relationship and had a four-year-old son. She had placed a contraceptive device in her arm two years prior with the intention of avoiding pregnancy.

At presentation in my clinic, she complained about generalized abdominal pain but denied any nausea or vomiting. She did not complain of any movement in her abdomen. Also, because of the contraceptive device that was in place, she could not readily identify the date of her last menstrual period.

Routine tests, including urine pregnancy tests, were negative. I treated her with Tylenol and nonsteroidal anti-inflammatory drugs (NSAIDS) but without any resolution of her abdominal cramps. I decided to do an ultrasound of her abdomen.

Six Months Pregnant and Not Aware

R. S. had the ultrasound, and the results were not what anybody had expected. The ultrasound revealed she had a healthy, six-month, male fetus! She had been pregnant for six months and was not even aware of it.

Immediate arrangements were made to take out the contraceptive device in her arm and begin basic obstetric medical protocols on this second trimester baby that had gone underneath the surveillance radar of urine pregnancy tests and physical exams.

At term, R. S. had a safe delivery. She delivered a ten-pound baby boy vaginally. Mummy and baby did well. She was apprehensive about what her months of unawareness might have caused the baby, but she trusted God to restore the lost time. Her miraculous pregnancy was found late in the Gregorian timetable, but it was not too late for God's timetable. Hallelujah!

Life lesson 20: God's timetable is always on time.

God called you to show evidence,
not speak explanations.

Chapter Twenty-One

Twenty-Four-Hour Miracle

How God anointed Jesus of Nazareth with the Holy Ghost and
with power: who went about doing good, and healing all that
were oppressed of the devil; for God was with him.
—Acts 10:38

M rs. A. S. (not her real name) came into the prayer meeting downcast and with shoulders drooping. She had just returned from a visit with her doctor that seemed to spell her possible doom.

According to her primary care physician, she had an abnormal mammogram highly suggestive of breast cancer. He suggested she follow up with a surgeon and schedule a breast biopsy for confirmation of his worst fears.

It was in that state of mind that A. S. walked into the Holy Ghost Night in April 2013. It was her first time visiting, but it would not be her last. A chance invitation had aroused her inquisitiveness. She came knowing that only God could change her story.

It's Gone!

During prayer and ministration, the visiting minister asked A. S. to come forward for prayer. By divine revelation, he told her that she had just been diagnosed with a disease but that God was going to heal her.

A. S. was stunned. Having been reared in a traditional Christian orthodox background and knowing fully well that no one could have informed the minister about her condition, she received the Word of knowledge as the power of God came upon her.

She followed up with her referral to the breast surgeon twenty-four hours later. He informed her that there was something in the previous mammogram but that there was nothing in the current mammogram. He could find no suitable scientific explanations for the difference and just kept saying, "It's gone."

A. S. has had no return of symptoms for breast cancer and is walking in divine, supernatural health. She attributes the anointing of the Holy Spirit as the source of her twenty-four-hour miracle!

Life lesson 21: Nothing is immoveable, and no condition permanent with the unchanging changer.

*One word from God can
change everything.*

Chapter Twenty-Two

Blind Eyes Burst Open

He sent his word, and healed them, and delivered them from their destructions.
—Psalm 107:20

O. M. (not his real name) came to the crusade grounds in Eastern Nigeria with expectation. He believed God would provide supernatural healing of his infirmed body and blind eyes as he waited unabatedly for the morning medical mission to finish.

The cost of treating his eyes would be enormous, and there was no medical solution readily available. He had been blind as a result of an infection. As a result, he had to be continuously escorted to the crusade grounds by some kindhearted women.

He had lost significant weight in the last two years and looked wasted. His cheekbones were protruding, his eyes were darkened, and his countenance was ominous. He could do nothing by himself, and his faith was the only glimmer of hope he had.

Drop That Stick and Walk!

As O. M. came forward for prayer, the evangelist cursed death in his body. He prophesied life in him, saying there was death on him but the resurrection power of the Holy Spirit would now spring forth.

Unaware of his blindness, the counseling team sent O. M. back to his seat. I, however, asked him to drop his stick and run to prove his healing. As he ran toward me without the cane, the crowd surged and exclaimed! One of the local pastors then revealed to me by that O. M. had not walked independent of a cane for nearly twenty years and was completely blind.

He surged forward and even grabbed me, attesting to the healing of his body in general and his eyes in particular. He counted single digits on my right hand and went home praising God for His wonder-working power.

Life lesson 22: Age is just a number, and disease is just a name in God's vocabulary.

Evidence is the end
of explanation.

Chapter Twenty-Three

What Kind of Woman Is This?

Come unto me, all ye that labor and are heavy laden, and I will give you rest.
—Matthew 11:28

T. O. (not her real name) is a thirty-nine-year-old African-American female who showed up at my clinic frantic and frustrated. Uninsured, she brought films of the mammogram she had had done six months earlier and wanted a solution to the mass burgeoning through her right breast.

Her mother had died from breast cancer as a young mother, and T. O. was the oldest of five girls. Her aunt had also died of breast cancer at a young age, and the signs and symptoms were ominous for metastatic breast cancer.

On examination, the right breast looked like a thickened red sauce on a light-brown surface. I referred her to surgical oncologists, and a biopsy confirmed my clinical suspicions. She had inflammatory breast cancer with metastatic deposits in the spine or liver and had a life expectancy of less than six months.

At age thirty-nine, T. O. was just starting life. She had two young girls, ages nine and seven, and had recently separated from her spouse. She worked as a schoolteacher and faced the daily struggles of life as a single mother.

In the midst of all this turmoil and medical terror, T. O. comported herself with extraordinary calm. She said, "No matter what happens,

I do not want my children to see me afraid or fretful." She underwent a radical mastectomy of the right breast and is currently undergoing chemotherapy and radiation therapy.

Is That a Baby Moving or What?

T. O. was undergoing a computer tomography (CT) scan of the abdomen when the radiologist noticed a fetus moving in her uterus. She had, in the midst of all her turmoil, been unaware she had missed her period and was pregnant.

The surgeons and radiologists were aghast and asked, "What kind of woman is this?" She was three months pregnant and unaware of it. The pregnancy, unfortunately, had to be aborted due to her medical condition and the complications that could arise from therapeutic interventions in her case.

She underwent chemotherapy, hormonal therapy, and radiation therapy after surgery. She is more than twelve months post-treatment and remains in stable health for a disease whose prognosis is usually less than twelve months. She has returned to work as school teacher and continues to exude a calm and confidence in God's grace that baffles human understanding.

Life lesson 23: A sign is God's signature, and a wonder is His welcome.

When Jesus says yes,
nobody can say no.

Chapter Twenty-Four

From Tremors to Testimonies

*And they overcame him by the blood of the Lamb, and by the word of
their testimony; and they loved not their lives unto the death.*
—Revelation 12:11

A. R. (not his real name) is an ardent member of the Assembly
West Monroe. Our families came to know each other from our
interaction in the Sunday school class called Relentless, which
Andy and Janice Varino led.

He suffered greatly from involuntary tremors of the body
(Parkinson's disease) and unusual spasms of the prostate that made it
impossible for him to voluntarily urinate.

He had been to several doctors without improvement. While I was
teaching about the supernatural power of God in Sunday school, he
and his lovely wife felt compelled to give my practice a trial.

He had been in and out of hospitals for months on end. He was
desperate for a solution. I prayed for him at the Sunday school and
felt God wanted to heal him permanently. In my clinic, I asked God
for supernatural wisdom to resolve his condition, and God supplied it!

Healed, Happy, and Holy

A. R. had been a pastor in his earlier years and wanted more than
anything to minister. His uncontrollable tremors, however, made it a
difficult task to coordinate preaching, teaching, and counseling.

After I treated him with God-inspired therapeutic interventions, including medications and referrals, A. R. has been back on the preaching circuit. He is actively involved in the church as an usher, and best of all, the tremors are almost unidentifiable.

Instead of wearing urinary catheters or running incessantly for the bathroom, A. R. now has a stable urinary stream. The intervention of God on our human efforts turned his captivity around.

In spite of his ordeal, A. R. was always in church, listening attentively and speaking openly about our possibilities in God and the power of God to accomplish whatever He called us to. Today, he is a witness of that power. Praise God!

Life lesson 24: Do not change your story to fit history, but fit history into His story for your life.

*If what you are obtaining
does not cost you something,
check its quality.*

Chapter Twenty-Five

Power of a Praying Mother

*Blessed is the man that feareth the L*ORD*, that delighteth greatly
in his commandments. His seed shall be mighty upon earth: the
generation of the upright shall be blessed. Wealth and riches shall
be in his house and his righteousness endureth for ever.*
—Psalm 112:1–3

D. F. (not her real name) became my patient fortuitously. While standing in front of my newly opened clinic, I waved at a couple passing in their car. The couple were local pastors, and through them, I was introduced to others, including D. F.

She had a long list of problems, but at the top of the list were issues concerning her oldest daughter. This daughter had had a baby at age sixteen outside of wedlock, and fifteen years later, she still had not had another child.

Although D. F. had married the man of her dreams ten years before I met her, she was facing a marriage that was on the rocks because another woman was involved. On top of all this, D. F's first grandson had been born premature and was plagued with uncontrollable seizures.

The God of All Possibilities

Notwithstanding these circumstances, D. F. kept praying for her daughter and grandson. Eighteen years after her initial conception, D. F's daughter gave birth to another baby, a healthy, bouncing boy.

Not to be outdone, D. F.'s grandson—who had recalcitrant seizures—was offered admission to a top medical college following a string of excellent grades.

The marriage between D. F.'s daughter and her husband that was teetering on the rocks has been restored. The recalcitrant seizures suffered by D. F.'s grandson are fast becoming a thing of the past as he gets ready for life as a college student.

D. F. knew her God was faithful and never quit believing God for her breakthrough. She persisted and eventually prevailed because she understood the power of a praying mother and grandmother.

Life lesson 25: Reaching out to God will restrict the Devil in your life.

*The word oops doesn't exist
in God's dictionary.*

Chapter Twenty-Six

High Calcium, High Cost, and Home Currently

For he doth not afflict willingly nor grieve the children of men. To crush under his feet all the prisoners of the earth, to turn aside the right of a man before the face of the most High (and) to subvert a man in his cause, the Lord approves not.
—Lamentations 3:33–34

R. U. (not his real name) was in his midthirties; for the three years he had been incarcerated, he had been doing well physically. But then he started complaining of recurrent itching and chest pain of sudden onset. After routine laboratory investigations were done, R. U. showed elevated calcium levels.

He saw several doctors, but he was not faring any better. When I took over his management as a physician in the penitentiary, he had very high levels of calcium, and it was getting worse.

I referred him to the tertiary care center in the area where he was diagnosed with non-Hodgkin lymphoma. The center subsequently administered chemo and radiation therapy, and his health improved.

His spiritual health also improved from our interaction as I shared the good news of Jesus Christ with him. He gave his life to Jesus and became a born-again believer in Jesus Christ.

A Prisoner Discharged as a Patient

In his few months of therapy, however, R. U. had accumulated hospital charges of nearly $1 million. The prison system considered his charge inconsistent with a lengthy sentence, especially in the light of his failing health. They asked for a quick parole instead.

From his hospital bed, R. U. was discharged home not as a prisoner but as a patient. The doctors caring for him said they had never witnessed a patient who had come in a prisoner and had left the hospital freely as a patient. R. U. was a one-in-a-million case!

He finished his treatment from home and is currently cancer- and prison-free! God turned not only his health around but also his life circumstances as well. God does not do some things well; He "does all things well" (Mark 7:37), and wherever you need Him, He will come through.

Life lesson 26: What God does for one, He can do for all.

You may be broken and bruised, but you can never be broken beyond God's repair.

Chapter Twenty-Seven

Bruised, Broken, but Blessed

A bruised reed shall he not break, and the smoking flax shall he not quench:
he shall bring forth judgment unto truth. He shall not fail nor be discouraged,
till he have set judgment in the earth and the isles shall wait for his law.
—Isaiah 42:3–4

R. Z. (not her real name) had an adorable son with her live-in lover. They were coming to church at the Assembly West Monroe, but they still had several areas of their lives they needed to surrender to God.

They were living together without being married and had already had one child. Their relationship had its share of "hiccups," and she shared many with me, her doctor.

One day however, R. Z. walked into my consulting clinic with a big gash across her right eye. She claimed she had fallen and had hurt herself, but as I was spurred on by the Holy Spirit, I insisted on her telling me the truth about her shiner.

I Can Do All Things through Christ

R. Z. broke down in tears and started pouring out her heart to me. She confessed that her baby's father had hit her but conceded she was the cause and asked me not to call the police. I assured her of my cooperation and my determination to raise the issue with her baby's father at the soonest.

I saw him the following Sunday morning at service, and he confessed his failing and his desire to become a better father and partner for his son and girlfriend respectively. I prayed for him and asked God to heal him of his insecurities and fill him with the love of God.

In less than a year, R. Z. and her baby's father married. She started a profession as a medical office staffer after having completed nine months of training. She and her husband are Christian parents rearing their son in the fear of the Lord.

Life lesson 27: There is no bruise beyond redemption and no case beyond Christ.

It is a probability, not a mere possibility, that a believer will obtain healing in Christ.

Chapter Twenty-Eight

Rejected, Raised Up, and Restored

But if the Spirit of him that raised up Jesus from the dead dwell
in you, he that raised up Christ from the dead shall also quicken
your mortal bodies by his Spirit that dwelleth in you.
—Romans 8:11

E. B. (not his real name) had just been abandoned by his wife of seventeen years when I met him as a patient. He was heartbroken and in a fragile state of health as a result.

He testified that even though he loved her, she had never really loved him. She, according to him, went to bed crying every night, wishing she had married another man.

In this rejected state of mind, his body also declined in health. He came into my office complaining of severe chest pains on two occasions. After due diligence and a thorough clinical examination, I sent him to the nearby hospital's emergency room.

On both occasions, he was rejected and dismissed as having noncardiac symptoms. On the third occasion of his having similar symptoms, I decided to send him to another community hospital in the area for evaluation.

I Stopped Breathing

E. B. was not discharged on this occasion but was sent to the cardiac lab for cardiac catheterization and possible stent placement. While he was undergoing the procedure on the catheterization table, his heart went into an irregular rhythm called ventricular fibrillation.

He momentarily became unconscious but woke up to see paddles on his chest and staff nurses administering cardiopulmonary resuscitation (CPR) on him. He knew he had just had a close encounter with death. They completed the stent placement, and because he had a greater than 70 percent main artery occlusion, they sent him home three days later.

He would have died if he had not changed medical facilities, and only the mercy of God and the astute acumen of the medical staff saved his life. As a result of that experience, he went from feeling rejected by his ex-wife to being restored. He began to see his life not as burden but as a blessing to humanity.

Life lesson 28: One wrong decision can make for lifelong destruction.

God made you a creator;
don't die a consumer.

Chapter Twenty-Nine

A Family Delivered from Disease, Discord, and Debt

If two of you shall agree on earth as touching any thing that they shall ask, it shall be done for them of my Father which is in heaven.
—Matthew 18:19

R. R. (not his real name) was three when I saw him. He had soft dimples and an average build, but beneath those physical attributes were disease and discord.

R. R. had a chronic case of elevated blood pressure considered malignant or of end-organ damaging potential due to a vessel-hardening disease in his rheumatologic system. Due to this, R. R. was placed on five antihypertensive medications.

While he was in the hospital, his father had been incarcerated for defaulting on several debts. Also, R. R. had been forcibly taken away from his mother for child protection reasons and placed under the care of a foster mother.

Turnaround Breakthrough

When I saw R. R., he had just been discharged from the hospital and was crestfallen and sulking. His new foster mother tried to provide a satisfactory environment that would mimic home, but he still wanted his home.

He was in no obvious discomfort when he came to my office for blood pressure monitoring. He had suffered a stroke when he was one, and referrals to pediatric neurologists, cardiologists, and nephrologists were made.

In the interim, the courts adjudicated that R. R. stay with his maternal grandmother and begin attending prekindergarten.

Pray for My Son

Meanwhile, when I was preaching at a nearby prison to a large group of men, I met R. R.'s father. He had come at the end of the service to ask for prayer for his son, and it was R. R!

We agreed in prayer for R. R., and on his next visit, his blood pressure was normal. His countenance had improved, and he exuded more joy.

I believe that God made my path cross R. R.'s father's path and that when we prayed the prayer of agreement, God broke the spell of disease, debt, and discord that had bound that family.

R. R.'s father is now out of jail and he has become reacquainted with his family. The health and social maladies R. R. faced have been obliterated by the power in the name of Jesus.

Life lesson 29: You cannot give what you do not have, and you cannot have what you do not give.

Grace is more than we deserve
and greater than we imagine.

Chapter Thirty

Established by Grace

For the LORD hath called thee as a woman forsaken and grieved in spirit,
and a wife of youth, when thou wast refused, saith thy God. For a small
moment have I forsaken thee; but with great mercies will I gather thee.
—Isaiah 54:6–7

R. X.'s (not her real name) abusive husband assaulted her continually. Although they had two children together, R. X. decided to run away from him to be safe. While in the process of escaping from him, someone at a train station in Illinois raped her.

She fled to Louisiana and soon learned she was having a daughter as a result of the sexual assault. R. X. had a safe and normal delivery. She married twice in her twelve years in Louisiana but without ever finding true love or success after the wedding altar.

In 2011, her mother kidnapped two children from her and kept them in underground cells without outside exposure for almost a year. The police eventually found and freed them and subsequently reunited them with R. X. She, however, had to disprove her mother's assertion that she was incapable of looking after her children and an unfit mother. She was nervous wreck and was in a state of panic and anxiety all day long. R. X. was a professional paralegal at a prominent law firm in the city, but as her health worsened, she lost her job due to declining productivity.

Overcoming Trauma, Terror, and Troubles

R. X., out of her wounds, began a ministry targeted at helping hurting women such as she was who were victimized by society and their spouses. She has a more stable health portfolio and is not as paranoid and anxious as she used to be.

Her children are in college pursuing degrees in accounting and business. Her children are mentally astute, and even the child who was the product of the rape has grown up beautifully without searching for her "dark" past or her unknown father.

R. X. has reconciled with her mother and looks for the parting of the skies to depart this world. She believes that the end game of life is not to be a wet blanket, always asking others for prayers and encouragement, but to encourage yourself and be a blessing to the world.

Life lesson 30: Brokenheartedness is a disease that has only one specialist physician—Jesus.

What you lose is what you kept, and what you gained is what you gave.

Chapter Thirty-One

Abdominal Pain, Anxiety, and the Anointing

Jesus of Nazareth, a man approved of God among you by miracles and wonders and signs, which God did by him in the midst of you.
—Acts 2:22

R. U. (not her real name) came to see me at the beginning of the school year complaining of severe abdominal pain. When she had these pains, she was unable to focus in class and had thrice, as a result, had to be rushed to the emergency room.

She had been on antianxiety and antidepressant medications as a result of a long history of bullying and pervasive violence in her prior school. Previous to her seeing me, her condition had been deemed the result of anxiety.

However, she was getting progressively worse. In the space of one month, she lost ten pounds. Her mental health medications were not ameliorating her condition and, as a result of being a member of the Assembly, she was referred to me for further assistance with the condition.

This Is the Devil

R. U. was a happy-go-lucky and full-of-life girl with no obvious signs of depression or anxiety. On examination, I felt concerned enough to order a scope of her upper and lower intestines. Her results returned negative, and I started her on antispasmodic and antireflux medications.

Her abdominal pain improved on the medications, but she persisted in atypical abnormal abdominal cramps at odd times. I advised her parents to increase her dosage of the medications until she had reached the maximum prescribed.

At the point that medicine had reached its limit, R. U. was still not well. I prayed in agreement with her mother that the abdominal pain would cease. In less than a week, R. U. told her mother she was pain-free. She affirmed to her parents that it was all a ruse of the Devil!

She still remains pain-free today and is fully active in school and church. The cause of her anxiety and abdominal pain was destroyed by the anointing of the Holy Spirit.

Life lesson 31: Calling things that are not as though they were will make them become what God calls them.

*Sexual sin is the only sin
God personally supervises
your punishment for.*

Chapter Thirty-Two

Healed of HIV and Haughtiness

God resisteth the proud, but giveth grace unto the humble.
—James 4:6

U. V. (not her real name) was the last child of a couple that, at the time of her birth, were involved in prostitution, pornography, and procuring illicit sex for high-class clients. As she grew, she witnessed her father physically abuse her mother several times. Her entire childhood was scarred by arguments and malevolent behavior. By her thirteenth birthday, U. V. had already had more than one abortion.

She refused to stay in school and had to be transferred from one state to the other to continue her education. At the time, she was estranged from God and was content with doing things her own way.

Denial, Deliverance, and Dumbed Down

At age fifteen, U. V. went on a three-day jamboree with a neighbor's son, and for the entire time she was there, nobody knew her whereabouts. She returned unapologetic but got the rudest shock of her life on evaluation in my office a few months later.

U. V. had, in that short space of time contracted HIV. She was in denial when I told her the diagnosis. She cried, wailed, and asked God for forgiveness. We agreed in prayer for the healing power of God to be manifest in her life, and God turned her captivity around.

Her labs were repeated to determine the HIV viral load. Against all usual calculations, her viral load came back insignificant and marginally above the lowest possible level.

She started antiretroviral treatment and is no more the wisecracking I-know-it-all girl I met before her diagnosis. She is dumbed down secularly but wiser spiritually.

Life lesson 32: Today's decisions are tomorrow's mistakes or miracles.

Practice makes perfect, so keep saying and doing until you see it.

Chapter Thirty-Three

The Massacre of the Mass in a Lung

Death and life are in the power of the tongue and they
that love it shall eat the fruit thereof.
—Proverbs 18:21

A. S. (not her real name) suffered with lung cancer for nearly two years. She underwent radical excision of the lung mass, chemotherapy, and radiation therapy. Even when medicine gave up and she was told she would be dead in six months, she refused to let cancer kill her.

She entered hospice care but outstayed hospice. Most hospice patients die within six months, but at two years, she was still thriving. She would come in to my clinic emaciated and short of breath but would always repeat her confession that Jesus is her healer and cancer would not have the final say on her health.

Her brothers and sisters watched her battle against the odds; they were amazed at her strength and positive mentality to live. A. S.'s cancer usually kills within six months at best, but three years later, A. S. was still alive.

Repetition Brings Re-Creation

A. S. had a chest wall such as I had never seen before. The chest wall cavity was disfigured by the lung cancer as it protruded through the wall. On a monthly basis during her visits, I laid hands on her and commanded healing on her body.

She never spoke a negative word; her words were always positive and uplifting even when every circumstance around her was negative. She believed she was healed and behaved as if she had a hundred years to live.

She never spoke about leaving earth or about what her burial preparations would be; she spoke only about life. Her mass was still protruding, but A. S. stood on God's message of hope and not despair.

She walked with such hope and carried herself with such confidence and assurance that she inspired others around her. While medical science gave her three months to live, A. S. has lived for three years because she loves and speaks life, not death.

Life lesson 33: "He that will love life, and see good days, let him refrain his tongue from evil, and his lips that they speak no guile. Let him eschew evil, and do good; let him seek peace, and ensue it" (1 Peter 3:10).

PART IV

Healing Lives—Personnel

If death was the end of your life, then you never really lived.

Chapter Thirty-Four

Still Waters Run Deep

Let me die the death of the righteous, and let my last end be like his.
—Numbers 23:10

G. B. (not his real name) was my mentor of sorts. A forerunner of my ministerial experience in Louisiana and an ardent worshipper at The Assembly West Monroe, he encouraged my wife and me to settle in Monroe and establish our ministry there.

He was unassuming and, on the surface, very gentle. He was a consummate tactician who believed one must plan not to fail if one wants to avoid failure.

He was married, had three lovely children, and he was the oldest son of his elderly parents. As a principal partner of a health care company and a health care provider himself, life was good—until cancer struck!

The Death of the Righteous

In life and in death, G. B. was impactful. He was diagnosed with hepatocellular carcinoma at age forty-three, and within four months was dead as a result.

He fought the fight gallantly and never acquiesced to any signs of weakness in front of his children. On the last day of his life, after having been discharged from a cancer institution, he died in the emergency room of a hospital.

While everyone involved was distraught and disillusioned, the nurse in the ER noted something no one else had noticed. G. B. had a big, beautiful smile on his face. He had died the death of the righteous and had made his life count to the end.

Life lesson 34: Life is not measured by its duration but by its donation to a cause.

Make your conversation edifying, not exterminating.

Chapter Thirty-Five

Against All Odds

So I prophesied as he commanded me, and the breath came into them, and
they lived, and stood up upon their feet, an exceeding great army.
—Ezekiel 37:10

U. M. (not her real name) was a close family friend and physician in the community. Our families had known each other for more than thirty years and were always looking out for each other.

In the summer of 2011, U. M. traveled to Nigeria and suffered a ghastly motor vehicle accident. According to the doctors who admitted her following the accident, her left hip was badly fractured and the bone was exposed. It would be near improbable, from the extent of her injury, for her to regain full use of that limb according to their medical expertise.

After the surgery, U. M. became worse. Her compound fracture was spreading infection in her body. Against medical advice, her husband transferred her to the United States for continued medical care.

On arrival, she immediately underwent a corrective repair of what had been done in Nigeria and was placed on nonweight-bearing wheelchair confinement. She later underwent three more surgeries in different hospitals in the United States that gave her a slim chance of full recovery.

Let These Bones Live

On my first visit with U. M. and her family after her return, I told her that God would heal her in a year and that she would be made whole. She received my words wholeheartedly and even quipped about God doing it in a shorter time period.

Her attitude throughout this trying period was exemplary. Even though she couldn't work, drive, or take care of her family because of the encumbrances of the fracture and the subsequent surgeries, she never whimpered or lost faith in God.

She spent time reading her Bible and daily chronicling her struggles. She recalls prophesying to her bones, as Ezekiel did in Ezekiel 37 when he faced very dry bones. She kept trusting God to breathe His breath on her bones.

In less than a year and against all medical and scientific odds, U. M. regained full use of her lower extremities. The orthopedic surgeon handling her case says her bones have been completely restored and she can return to full activity.

Today she is back at work, runs her own pediatric office, and is working on a book titled *Against My Body*. The book documents her experience during some dark moments of despair and how God restored her to a victorious place of health. She can testify truly that Jesus is a healing Jesus!

Life lesson 35: Freedom is not a function of physical liberty but of spiritual insight.

Moderation is not mediocrity.

Chapter Thirty-Six

From Blindness to Beauty and Brains

And they were all amazed, and they glorified God, and were filled
with fear, saying, We have seen strange things to day.
—Luke 5:26

R. M. (not her real name) is a Christian clinical psychologist. She was born legally blind, and the numerous specialists she consulted gave her no chance at gaining normal vision. She was told that she had a rare disorder culminating in calcification of the optic arteries and that there was no medical or surgical solution. The best ophthalmologists in the country advised her parents to train her in Braille because of her inevitable loss of vision.

In their eyes, she was confined to a life of mediocrity because of her disability and nothing could change that situation. At age five, however, something happened that changed R. M's worldview.

My Miracle Patient

R. M. woke up one morning at age five with clear vision. The halos and the blurry images were gone, and she could appreciate differences in color, shape, and size clearly.

It was nothing short of a miracle. Her doctors were astounded at her sudden and positive change; they could find no scientific explanation.

At age eighteen, she recalls seeing one of her eye physicians at a symposium. He referred to her as his "miracle patient' who defied all the medical odds to see again.

Not content with just right sight, R. M. obtained a doctorate in family therapy and counseling as is a licensed clinical psychologist. She leads a formidable Christian counseling network in her church; God has used her to transform the lives of so many "down and outers."

R. M. attributes her faith in Christ as the conduit for the miracles that have berthed at her shore in life. She describes herself as a recipient of divine grace and not an achiever of anything elusive. She is humble and moderate and has unequivocally shown that life in Christ does not need to be mediocre.

Life lesson 36: From reversals to revivals, it is all God-sourced.

You cannot transform the world if you conform to it.

Chapter Thirty-Seven

Turnaround Testimony

As for you, ye thought evil against me; but God meant it unto good,
to bring to pass, as it is this day, to save much people alive.
—Genesis 50:20

R. D. (not his real name) was a classmate of mine in medical school. His father was a well-to-do bank manager, and everything was going smoothly in his home, in which he was the eldest of three children.

Suddenly everything fell apart. R. D.'s father decided on taking a second wife, which is legal in Nigeria. R. D.'s mother resisted spiritually by praying for him to change his mind, but R. D.'s father persisted.

He became callous toward the family's needs and turned a blind eye to their welfare. R. D.'s mother had to do cleaning jobs and other menial jobs to see him through medical school while his father doted on his new wife and her children. R. D. saw his mother's pain and wanted recompense for her.

He graduated from medical school and traveled abroad with the intention of showing his gratitude in the future to his mother. Unfortunately, one day while coming from work, she had a heart attack and died. R. D. was devastated, and his world was thrown into confusion.

More Than We Can Imagine

While his mom was alive, she had witnessed to R.D. and had asked him to secure his life by salvation in Christ. After her death, he became an infectious disease specialist, married a cardiologist, had a daughter, and most important, gave his life to Jesus.

His sisters won a visa that enabled them to relocate to the United States. R.D., who looked as if he had lost his family when he had moved to the United States, suddenly had his family around him again.

He still harbored unforgiveness toward his dad, however. He knew he needed healing in his spirit from bitterness and vengefulness. He asked God to heal him of those paternal bruises he had endured much of his life. God did!

He saw his father ten years after his mother's death and told him he loved him. He also forgave the second wife, who had disenfranchised his mother from the home. He welcomed her children as his stepbrothers and sisters and reached out to assist them in any way he could.

God has given R. D. more than he could ever have imagined, and because God had forgiven him, he forgave his father. Mark 11:24–25: "What things soever ye desire, when ye pray, believe that ye receive them, and ye shall have them. And when ye stand praying, forgive, if ye have ought against any."

Life lesson 37: Emotional cargo leads to spiritual embargo.

*God is more willing to answer
than we are to pray.*

Chapter Thirty-Eight

Destroying the Destroyer

For this purpose the Son of God was manifested, that
he might destroy the works of the devil.
—1 John 3:8

C ancer has become the great destroyer of modern mankind. It has or is estimated in the near future to overtake cardiovascular disease as the number-one cause of death in the world.

When my staff, D. R. (not her real name) found a mass in her armpit, she feared the worst. She underwent a biopsy of the mass, and the results confirmed her worst fears.

She was told she had stage IV carcinoma that would benefit from chemotherapy. She needed further tests, however, to ascertain the source. She called me and asked for my wife and me to pray for her.

We prayed for her as a congregation at the Holy Ghost Night prayer meetings, earnestly asking God for her healing. She had a young family, was in her early fifties, and was not ready to let go of her life.

Cancer Can't Be Found

D. R. underwent a colonoscopy, the removal of both breasts, and endometrial biopsy in an attempt to find the source of the cancer. Even though the oncologists had tissue confirmation of her cancer, they were reluctant to start chemotherapy until they had a definitive origin.

All their tests, surgical and radiological, came back blank. They could not detect a trace of cancer in D. R. The doctors were puzzled and postponed the chemotherapy indefinitely.

D. R., who had planned to be absent from work for four to five months because of treatment complications, wrote to my administration asking to return to work within three months.

She was eventually put on chemotherapy for innocuous cancer but has returned with strength and vigor to her old job, singing songs of God's miraculous healing and salvation, Cancer dies in the presence of Jesus because "by His stripes we were healed" (1 Peter 2:24).

Life lesson 38: Cancer is just another name that bows at the name of Jesus.

Those who violate hell are the violent, not the volatile.

Chapter Thirty-Nine

Stroked Out by a Witch but Healed by Jesus

As the bird by wandering, as the swallow by flying,
so the curse causeless shall not come.
—Proverbs 26:2

D r. Oguine was in the middle of a busy clinic on a hot afternoon when a woman came into his obstetric practice in Aba, Southeast Nigeria. It was the late 1980s, and he had just returned from Canada, where he had undergone specialist training in obstetrics and gynecology.

A gentleman to the core, Dr. Oguine asked this lady what he could do for her. She responded that she was experiencing uncontrollable vaginal bleeding and urgently wanted a consultation.

Dr. Oguine found her to be extremely anemic and with a very fast heart rate. He feared the worst and scheduled an immediate urgent exploratory surgery of her abdomen.

While he was wheeling her into the operating room, however, the woman told him that she was a witch and that he should not operate on her if he didn't want to die. He dismissed her threat as a result of her worsening anemia and prepped her for surgery.

The Curse Is Broken

Dr. Oguine finished the surgery successfully and, while driving home, became paralyzed. He lost movement and feeling in the right side of his body. He didn't relate it to the self-confessed "witch" he had operated on and discharged her from his hospital a week later.

His wife and family took him to a prayer meeting, where men of God in Nigeria prayed for him, and he was restored to full health. Two weeks later, however, this "witch" called him; after he had spoken with her, his symptoms came back.

He went to the best rehabilitation and neurological physicians in the country, but no one could improve or even ameliorate his condition. He rapidly went downhill, and two years after the commencement of this malaise, he turned his heart to Jesus, asking for forgiveness of sins and healing.

He became an ardent student of the Word of God, and even though he had always been a religious individual and had a wife and children (classmates of mine in medical school) who believed in the uncompromising power of faith, he needed to believe God for himself.

Dr. Oguine eventually received ministrations of healing and deliverance by several pastors and regained use of the right side of his body. His speech was restored, and he was even able to perform surgeries again. The curse of stroke had been broken by the power in the name of Jesus.

Dr. Oguine went on to leave a legacy of faith, family, and fortune to his community. He championed the cause of the defenseless and played a pivotal role in the establishment of the Aba, Nigeria chapter of the Full Gospel Business Men Fellowship International (FGBMFI).

He told everyone at every opportunity what a glorious Savior and healer Jesus was. He knew firsthand the power in the name of Jesus!

Life lesson 39: What Satan has is power of deception, not power to dominate.

Don't force God, fear God.

Chapter Forty

Paralyzed at Birth but Unlimited in Life

*But Jesus beheld them, and said unto them, With men this
is impossible; but with God all things are possible.*
—Matthew 19:26

D r. Ifeoma Nnaji is a family physician in the Atlanta, Georgia area. She was born healthy; but at an early age, she contracted polio. Because of the limited resources available in Nigeria at the time, she lost the full use of her legs and became a paraplegic.

She took up the gauntlet, however, and refused to be discouraged. In a country in which millions with similar conditions live on the fringes of society and make a living by begging, Ifeoma chose to become somebody of note to the glory of God.

She attained admission into the medical school at the University of Nigeria (where she and I were contemporaries). She was, however, asked to leave the school in her third year because of poor academic scores.

From Precipice to Pinnacle

Anyone else faced with the arduous physical, academic, and emotional challenges Ifeoma faced would have hung up their gloves and quit. Many would have taken the path of least resistance, but not Dr. Ifeoma Nnaji.

She decided to take the requisite examinations and transfer from the University of Nigeria to Cleveland University in Ohio. She was successful and went on to finish medical school at Morehouse Medical College. Along the way, she also obtained a master's in business administration.

As a final-year medical student, she interviewed with several obstetric and gynecological programs for residency admission. Unfortunately, her disability made her (on their terms) unsuitable for an obstetrics/gynecology practice. Consequently, she took up family medicine as a specialty.

Against the odds both at home and abroad, Ifeoma Nnaji has emerged as evidence that with God, all things are possible. She still has to walk with double crutches, and she wheelchairs around hospitals and consulting clinics. In spite of her handicap, she carries herself taller than people with a taller stature. Her being able to do so is because of who she believes in—Jesus.

Life lesson 40: Nothing can stop a man or woman in Jesus' company.

PART V

Healing Lives—Pastors

*God did not call you
to entertainment but
to attain to Christ.*

Chapter Forty-One

Stretching a Saint with a Cut Colon

Enlarge the place of thy tent, and let them stretch forth the curtains of thine habitations: spare not, lengthen thy cords, and strengthen thy stakes for thou shall break forth on the right hand and on the left.
—Isaiah 54:2–3

M. S. (not her real name) had just been diagnosed with colon cancer. It was 1995, and as a minister's wife and a pastor's daughter, she had read, preached, and knew all the Scriptures on healing. Now, however, she needed to believe them for herself.

M. S. underwent exploratory surgery at the hands of a Christian surgeon in the Louisiana Assembly of God district she belonged to. He cut out, according to his surgical report, three feet of colon and reconnected the remaining three feet of colon.

Every adult has an average of six feet of colon. In M. S.'s case, due to the surgery she underwent, she had only three feet left. However, when in six months she was reexamined by her gastroenterologist via a colonoscopy, he found six feet of colon in her!

Not only has the cancer disappeared and never returned, God reconstructed her damaged colon and gave her new body parts. Her faith and that of the doctors and others who knew about the case were stretched by this supernatural act.

Bilateral Breast Masses

M. S., in her sixties, had been cancer-free for eighteen years and was enjoying her best time in the ministry with her husband. They were rehabilitating foreign children who had suffered from lack of food and shelter and were equipping them, using the help of partners, with clothes, food, healthcare, and education.

In the midst of their activities, she had her routine annual exam. The screening mammogram suggested breast masses. She underwent biopsies on both breasts and, remembering the miracle of the stretched colon, stood on the Word of God and claimed His healing for her breasts.

Both breast biopsies returned with a verdict of benign tumors! Even though the magnetic resonance imaging (MRI) of the breasts and the mammograms had been equivocal in their identification of a malignant cancer, God intervened and changed what looked malignant into benign.

M. S. has thus twice been a victor in Christ over cancer. She believes God is not a respecter of persons, and the same one who has been rich in mercy unto her through the blood of His son Jesus can give anyone who asks and believes his or her own healing. Take it by faith. The impossible is probable and possible again in Jesus' name.

Life lesson 41: What the world considers impossible, God considers probable by faith.

God is able to take you from the guttermost to the uttermost if you make him your uppermost.

Chapter Forty-Two

From Drugs to Destiny

Wherefore he is able also to save them to the uttermost that come unto
God by him, seeing he ever lives to make intercession for them.
—Hebrews 7:25

E. W. (not his real name) is the senior pastor of a major denomination's branch church in Louisiana. He took up the reins of leadership from the then–deputy superintendent and was unanimously voted in as senior pastor.

Unknown to most of the congregation, however, was the past E. W. had lived and been redeemed from. He had spent eight years in the biggest prison in the country, Louisiana State Penitentiary, Angola, for drug charges and aggravated assault.

He had grown up in a dysfunctional home and had moved between several stepfathers and relatives but without a real father figure. He soon found solace in drugs and alcohol. At age thirteen, he began to peddle and use hard drugs.

By the time he reached thirty, he had been in and out of jail multiple times. To him, life seemed short and brutish with little or nothing for which to live.

In his midtwenties, he was arrested in a major drug bust and was sentenced to thirty years in Angola. At that point, holed up in an eight-by-six cell, he asked Jesus to come into his life and save him.

If God Gets Me Out of Here, I Will Serve Him Forever

He promised God that if He set him free, he would serve Him by preaching the gospel all the days of his life. He began a correspondence Bible course and became one of the most active Christian preachers in the prison.

Miraculously, he was granted an early pardon and remanded to a halfway house. In those three years, at the Christian themed halfway house, he worked as a maintenance man at the Assembly West Monroe.

He was subsequently appointed pastor of the largest youth group in Northeast Louisiana. Under E. W.'s leadership, the youth group quadrupled in size. As a result, he became a reference point in ministry for raising successful youth ministers. He completed his correspondence Bible courses and became an ordained minister in 2011.

While leading the students group, he met and fell in love with a psychology major student in the church. They got married in 2011, and in 2013, they welcomed their first child, a beautiful girl. Nearly twenty years after a lifetime of crime and drugs, E. W. is finally fulfilling destiny by the power in the blood of Jesus.

Life lesson 42: Never cast out anyone because in the outcasts of life are God's starring casts for life's master show.

Consumerism has turned the Creator into a commodity and the Lord of hosts into a label.

Chapter Forty-Three

From Insomnia to Irruption

*Be careful for nothing; but in every thing by prayer and supplication
with thanksgiving let your requests be made known unto God.
And the peace of God, which passeth all understanding, shall
keep your hearts and minds through Christ Jesus.*
—Philippians 4:6

A. W. (not her real name), alongside her husband, pastor one of the city of Monroe's fast-growing congregations, had been in ministry for a few years. When faced with some challenges, she developed insomnia and an elevated blood pressure.

She reported her complaints to her primary care physician, who prescribed more drugs for her. Her blood pressure did not get better, and her sleeplessness was worsening.

She asked about physicians, and someone in her ministry recommended my clinic and its services. When I saw her, she was distraught. The sleeplessness and high blood pressure had incapacitated her so much that she had streamlined her ministry obligations to the barest minimum. Her husband had come along with her, and they needed answers quickly!

Forget, Focus, and Forge Ahead

The first thing I did when she came to my clinic was to discard all her old medications. The Holy Spirit told me to start her on a new medication plan, and I obeyed.

A. W. and her husband were skeptical and wanted an explanation for the sudden change in medications. I told them the previous medications were undertreating the blood pressure and overworking her body for results.

In less than a month, she returned to my clinic, testifying that her blood pressure was normal, that her mood was stable, and that she had sweet sleep again. What had afflicted her for months dissolved as a result of one moment's obedience.

A. W. has since returned to the forefront of ministry and is enjoying life and ministry better than ever. She is expanding her ministry to radio and television and increasing in significance in the community.

Life lesson 43: Nothing worthwhile starts until you stop self and follow the Spirit of God.

Who is in you is greater than what you are in!

—Pastor Shane Warren,
The Assembly West Monroe

Chapter Forty-Four

Life without Limits

*If the Spirit of him that raised up Jesus from the dead dwell in
you, he that raised up Christ from the dead shall also quicken
your mortal bodies by his Spirit that dwelleth in you.*
—Romans 8:11

T
he surgeon had just told Rev. Ashbrook, the then–district
superintendent of the Louisiana area for the Assemblies of
God, that he had less than six months to live because he had
an inoperable lung mass and that the best of treatment would prolong
his life for only a year.

In that one moment, the revered gentleman and his wife faced
down the surgeon and told him that in the absence of a cure from
medicine or surgery, they would depend on God for his healing.

That was in the 1960s! Rev. Ashbrook lived another forty years
pastoring megachurches from Hong Kong to Louisiana without losing
a step. Even though his faith was severely challenged on several
occasions, he never quit. His son John remembers him coughing
up chunks of bloody sputum while on the pulpit but nevertheless
preaching till he ended his sermon.

Discovery: The Birthplace of Recovery

Rev. Ashbrook discovered a pivotal Scripture that changed his
health forever. He was preaching one day from Romans 8:11 when God

showed him the Holy Spirit in him could do what he needed—quicken his mortal body: "If the Spirit of him that raised up Jesus from the dead dwell in you, he that raised up Christ from the dead shall also quicken your mortal bodies by his Spirit that dwelleth in you" (Romans 8:11).

He lifted up his arms in surrender while at the meeting and began to claim that promise for his physical body. Over a period of years, his body was restored by the quickening power of the Holy Spirit, and he preached three services a Sunday while pastoring a chapel in Hong Kong.

As at the time of his passing at nearly age eighty, he had lived a fulfilled life and proven the Word of God. He was a healing life who walked where others feared to tread and accomplished more than legions of ordinary men do in their lifetimes.

Life lesson 44: Revelation is at the root of all breakthroughs.

The opportunity of a lifetime must be seized in the lifetime of that opportunity.
—Pastor Leonard Ravenhill (1907–1994)

Chapter Forty-Five

And Idahosa Died

For to me to live is Christ, and to die is gain.
—Philippians 1:21

T he late Archbishop Benson Idahosa was, in the mid 1970s' and 80s', involved in a well-publicized turf war with the dreaded Ogboni cult of Benin City. The members of the cult believed they owned the city of Benin and its environs, but the archbishop thought otherwise.

He believed, according to Revelation 11:15, that "the kingdoms of this world are become the kingdoms of our Lord, and of His Christ." He didn't believe he was just a subject of the royal palace but an occupier of the land (according to Luke 19:13).

When Idahosa returned to Benin City after his internship at the Christ for the Nations Bible College in Dallas, Texas, he found it had become commonplace to see hanging corpses of birds, animals, and humans on street corners in his home city; people were making sacrifices of them to the gods of the land.

Idahosa declared on television that he had unilaterally abolished the killing of human beings and the offering of sacrifices in Benin City. He pronounced a death sentence on any unrepentant witches and wizards, and the die was cast for a clash of civilizations in Benin City.

We Cannot Kill Him!

In response, the cult made death threats and attacked him physically and spiritually, but without success. Idahosa decided to relocate his church, Bible college, and residence to the most feared forest in Benin City.

The people believed evil spirits lived there, and living there was tantamount to death as it violated their space. To the contrary, Idahosa's church and ministry expanded globally. At a point, he was building a new church building every week and opening a branch every day.

He began the spiritual cleanup of Benin City, and at the turn of the century, when he died, he had transformed Benin City from a high-tempo witchcraft coven to a city in revival with the gospel of Jesus Christ.

Archbishop Benson Idahosa preached a sermon, "The gain of death," on the Sunday before he died. He also told every member of his congregation at that Sunday service that he had accomplished his mission on earth and had finished his assignment.

A great man never leaves unannounced. As He did with Elijah and Moses, God informs men and women of renown about their departure before the day comes. Archbishop Idahosa asked that that tape message "the gain of death" be circulated worldwide for his end had come, and two days later, he was taken in a blaze of glory while eating with guests from America.

His life is a healing life because he changed the spiritual landscape of a city dogged by the demagogues of witchcraft and sexual immorality. His legacy continues among his children, wife, church, staff, and students of Benson Idahosa University, Benin, Nigeria.

Life lesson 45: What you cannot cast out will become your lasting past.

You cannot have satanic patrol and walk in supernatural overflow.

Chapter Forty-Six

Murderer Muzzled

Behold, they shall surely gather together, but not by me: whosoever shall gather together against thee shall fall for thy sake.
—Isaiah 54:15

The senior pastor of Dunamis International Gospel Centre in Abuja, Nigeria Dr. Paul Enenche, is an indefatigable champion of the oppressed. A medical doctor, he has seen the church he and his wife started in 1996 multiply to tens of thousands of members across four continents. The church owns a television station and accommodates a plethora of educational facilities, including a Bible school and elementary school facilities.

He has multiplied testimonies of God's work in his congregation through healing, deliverances, and mighty miracles. He was recently elected the president of the Pentecostal Fellowship of Nigeria (PFN) in Abuja as a show of the confidence his peers have in him.

As his fortune increased, so did his enemies. Recently, an upper court in sentenced a driver, Yakubu Mohammed, to five months imprisonment for attempted murder of Pastor Paul Enenche. According to Mohammed, who admitted being a member of a secret cult with headquarters at the top of a rock, he had been assigned by the head of the cult to assassinate Pastor Enenche.

Assassination Annihilation

As Pastor Paul's enemies gathered, so did his spiritual defense forces. According to the testimony of Mohammed, an avowed ritualist and murderer, "I was fortified to carry out the mission, and I tried all I could to finish Pastor Paul Enenche, but my powers failed me completely. I had no option than to go to the church and confess." Mohammed, knowing God's supreme power was greater than his, confessed to Pastor Adetope James of the security department of the church. According to this man who claims to have killed scores of innocents, he had been monitoring Pastor Paul Enenche's movement since April 2013 and surveying the church premises for an opportunity to carry out his mission.

The anointing of God upon Pastor Paul Enenche protected him from occult, evil men around him. Every attack was supernaturally repelled by divine cover, and God was glorified.

Pastor Paul Enenche is a healing live because through his life, darkness has been extinguished and the evidence of God's Word in the area of protection and preservation is displayed.

Life lesson 46: Just as no fly can perch on a stove and survive, the Devil cannot touch a man or woman on fire for God and live.

Until the strange begins to happen in the church, the same will continue in the world.

Chapter Forty-Seven

Healed of Pancreatic Cancer

*Jesus looking upon them saith, With men it is impossible, but
not with God: for with God all things are possible.*
—Mark 10:27

E vangelist Jerry McGee is the president of freedom crusades
international. In his teenage and young adult years, he joined
a nefarious band of motorcycle riders, Hell's Angels, and
crisscrossed America, smoking drugs and worshipping the Devil.

He gave his life to Christ and God delivered him from alcohol,
women, drugs, and wayward living. He also was called into the ministry
as an evangelist/pastor. He served as pastor of several churches and
has shared his testimony with thousands around the world.

In the course of powerful worldwide revivals, he developed a total
loss of appetite. He soon after became jaundiced (yellow skin and
yellow eyes) and was throwing up everything he tried to eat.

He lost more than fifty pounds in less than two months. On
evaluation by his physician, he learned that he had a mass on the head
of his pancreas. His medical team counseled him to undergo invasive
surgery and chemotherapy that would add, at most, twelve months
to his life. The alternative was to go home and die within six months.
He chose neither!

Nothing but the Word

Jerry McGee's wife immediately countered the word of the doctor and told him Jerry would not die but live. They opined that if medicine had only twelve months to offer him, it would be better to trust God. The doctor called them foolhardy and warned them of the dire consequences of their action, but they insisted on God and God alone.

For seven days, Jerry and his wife shut themselves away from the outside world to seek and meditate on God's Word on healing. Jerry cancelled all his appointments and faced the God who can do what man calls impossible.

After the extended period of waiting on the Lord and considering His Almighty promises, Jerry represented himself to the physician who had told him he needed surgery. In shock and awe, that doctor testified that the tumor had disappeared and that Jerry was cancer-free.

All the tests were repeated, but not a single trace of pancreatic cancer was found. Fifteen years later, Evangelist Jerry McGee is healthy and strong. He crisscrosses continents proclaiming the healing gospel of Jesus not only as one alive by faith in Jesus but also as one given life again by the power of Jesus' name.

Life lesson 47: You may not know what tomorrow holds, but you know who holds tomorrow—God.

To go all out for God,
you have to go all in.
—Mark Batterson, pastor and author

Chapter Forty-Eight

The Birth of Elijah Olukoya

There shall nothing cast their young, nor be barren, in thy land:
the number of thy days I will fulfil. I will send my fear before thee,
and will destroy all the people to whom thou shalt come, and I
will make all thine enemies turn their backs unto thee.
—Isaiah 23:26–27

D r. D. K. Olukoya and his wife, Shade, stood on God's Word for fifteen years before they saw the birth of their son, Elijah. It was a long, arduous, and challenging time according to Dr. Olukoya.

He said that even though he pastored the largest church on the African continent and had seen multiple miracles and deliverances, the experience of childlessness was the most daunting to him.

Some people, he said, asked him to look outside Jesus, consult other gods, or at least merge forces to overcome the shame of childlessness, but he and his wife never budged. Rumor had it that their childlessness was the result of a covenant he had made with devils to grow his church.

He, however, knew that the God, who began the good work in them, would accomplish it in His time. In 2001, the inevitable happened! The manifestation of prophecy and Scripture was fulfilled as Elijah Olukoya was born and the Devil was put to shame.

Since his birth, the Mountain of fire and Miracles has increased in its global spread. It now has branches in every country in the world and accommodates nearly a million people at its monthly Power must change hands program. God is faithful.

Life lesson 48: Ultimate victory is commanded for those who fear God and who never stop believing.

When you think ahead of your enemy, you will live far above him or her.

Chapter Forty-Nine

Martyr in Maiduguri

They overcame him by the blood of the Lamb, and by the word of
their testimony; and they loved not their lives unto the death.
—Revelation 12:11

Maiduguri is a city in the northeastern part of Nigeria that is more than 99 percent Muslim. It is illegal there to convert to Christianity, and proselytizing is punishable by extrajudicial killing.

Maiduguri is also home to pastor S. T. (not his real name) and his church where he serves as church secretary. Neighboring Muslims vilified him for boldly preaching the gospel, and their propaganda eventually snowballed into hate crimes against pastor S. T.

One night, they invaded his home, clutching machetes and guns. They asked his wife and children to lie flat on the floor while pastor S. T. was asked to renounce his faith in Jesus Christ and confess Muhammad as the prophet of God or be shot dead.

At gunpoint, pastor S. T. refused to deny Jesus. He boldly told his assailants that Jesus is Lord and that no one else could save but Him. At that juncture, they put the gun to his cheek and pulled the trigger. Pastor S. T. fell to the ground, and the assassins disappeared into the dark night.

Shot but Not Ashamed

Miraculously, the bullet went from one cheek to the other without causing major harm. Pastor S. T. stood up as soon the criminals left, and assisted by his family, went to a nearby Christian hospital for treatment.

He underwent surgical repair and has regained full oral function since the traumatic incident. He stood up boldly for Christ because he was "not ashamed of the gospel of Christ [which is] the power of God unto salvation to every one that believeth" (Romans 1:16).

After the incident, Pastor S. T. has inspired several believers to stand in faith for what they believe. The God who shielded the three Hebrew children from the furnace of Nebuchadnezzar (see Daniel 3:19–27) is still at work today. Those who overcome walk in faith, not fear (1 John 5:4).

Life lesson 49: Nothing stops fear like faith in the right person or thing.

God is more interested in allegiance than acquaintance.

Chapter Fifty

Nothing Shall Be Impossible

Jesus said unto him, If thou canst believe, all things
are possible to him that believeth.
—Mark 9:23

E vangelist Chris Akosa was a regular preacher on our campus. He never told us he and his wife were experiencing difficulty conceiving; he just preached the gospel uncompromisingly and passionately on the power of God to make barren women fruitful. After almost fifteen years of marriage, he and his wife welcomed their son into the world.

He did not bemoan his situation, conduct pity parties, or turn his mountains into monuments. Rather, he spoke the Word of God uncompromisingly and obtained his miracle.

Total Turnaround

After the birth of their miracle son, Evangelist Chris and his wife adopted a girl. Their ministry is thriving, and Evangelist Chris has traveled to the United States and the United Kingdom in his ministry of the Word.

Evangelist Chris's wife resigned her job and started working with her husband as an evangelist/teacher. Since that decision, God has supplied all their needs according to His riches in Christ Jesus.

They have written about ten books since their decision to go into ministry full time and have supported the cause of many downtrodden orphans in the area. They also conduct a popular couples' conference quarterly that spurs couples to live for God.

Life lesson 50: Your dreams are a mind-set away from their delivery.

God is the anointer
without number.

Chapter Fifty-One

From Outcast to Overflow

They that sow in tears shall reap in joy. He that goeth forth
and weepeth, bearing precious seed, shall doubtless come
again with rejoicing, bringing his sheaves with him.
—Psalm 126:5–6

J oyce Meyer was born into a dysfunctional family. She was sexually abused in her teens by her alcoholic father. She divorced her first husband after he abandoned her at a California hotel five years after their marriage.

She tried to drown her sorrows in alcohol, drugs, and cigarettes until her spiritual rebirth, a salvation experience, when she was thirty-two. She remarried and began a Bible study in her congregation.

When the church board refused to give her permission to lead the Bible study, she moved to another church in St. Louis, Missouri, that allowed her to lead weekly Bible classes. It was from there that she rose to be assistant pastor.

Enjoying Everyday Life

That Bible study has since grown to become the nucleus of the "Enjoying Everyday Life" conferences and state-of-the-art studios from which daily broadcasts are transmitted globally.

She also established the Hand of Hope Outreach and the St. Louis Dream Center that caters to abused children and ostracized families.

157

Her family struggles gave her the impetus to tackle the struggle of single, abused women with her message of hope and love in Jesus Christ.

Her ministry currently tops the global ministry landscape with income totaling over $100 million annually. From a background of oppression and abuse, God has elevated her to be a voice to the world concerning what is possible when one overcomes rejection and reproach by coming to Christ. She hates her past enough to avoid going back to it and so lives in the overflow.

Life lesson 51: God can start your life and ministry at forty or later—so never quit!

*Who you join determines
what you enjoy.*

Chapter Fifty-Two

From Death to Life

Unto him that is able to do exceeding abundantly above all that
we ask or think, according to the power that worketh in us.
—Ephesians 3:20

A ngie and Tim Todd are members of the Assembly West Monroe and leaders of an international evangelistic ministry called "Revival Fires USA." In October 1995, Angie had a dream she had given birth to a stillborn daughter who was miraculously raised from the dead and named Miracle Joy.

The dream stirred the spirits of Angie and Tim Todd, but they were unaware they were about to face the most pivotal trial of their faith ever. Shortly after the dream, Angie became pregnant with twins and, following prenatal care, the twins were diagnosed as having twin-to-twin transfusion syndrome. Doctors concede that this condition, with a mortality rate of 95 to 100 percent, is incompatible with life. They urged the Todds to terminate the pregnancy. They told them that neither twin would be born alive and that it was futile keeping the pregnancy.

Miracle Joy

At this point, Angie's dream began to reappear in their consciousness, and they told the maternal-fetal specialist, "Both twins will live and not die. We will not terminate the pregnancy."

At thirty-one weeks of gestation, the babies were born by cesarean section. Mariah weighed two pounds fourteen ounces while Miracle Joy weighed only one pound and two ounces.

Miracle Joy remained in the hospital for six months, underwent six major surgeries, and was on a ventilator for the first year of her life. She eventually came home. Today, she is a senior in high school without any neurological or social deficits.

Life lesson 52: There is no hopeless situation when you meet the hope of the world—Jesus.

*The blessings of God qualify
the gift and not vice versa.*

Chapter Fifty-Three

From Cancer to Cured

Praise the LORD, O my soul, and forget not all his benefits—
who forgives all your sins and heals all your diseases.
—Psalm 103:2–3

D odie Osteen was diagnosed with liver cancer in December 1981. A terminal condition, this type of cancer gave her less than six weeks to live by human standards, but not by God's standards.

She and her late husband, Pastor John Osteen, locked themselves in for upward of six weeks to feed on healing Scriptures. She would speak them over herself again and again and agreed in prayer with her husband that she was healed.

When she came out of her spiritual solitude, she believed she was healed. She made it a point to forgive anyone she had hurt or had been hurt by. She was told by medical professionals to have the surgery or lose her life. Thirty-three years later, she is still alive, and the liver cancer has disappeared.

Far from Oppression

Dodie still prays, preaches, and pastors at Lakewood Church, which she and her husband founded more than forty years ago. After they told her to go home and prepare to die thirty-three years ago, Dodie is not just surviving but is thriving in ministry.

She shares her story of healing in the book *Healed of Cancer* and is the head of the prayer ministry at the new Lakewood Church pastored by her son Joel. She believes in ministering to others in prayer even during health challenges as that causes God to reward and restore what you may have lost (see Job 42:10).

Dodie's life is an example of what God can do when we call on Him and believe. She is currently in her eighties but still actively participates in the church her son leads. Her life is a testimony that God is real and the Devil is defeated!

Life lesson 53: Whatever people say, God always has the final say.

You can be too expensive
for the Devil to attack.

Chapter Fifty-Four

Better Than My Fathers

Write the things which thou hast seen, and the things which
are, and the things which shall be hereafter.
—Revelation 1:19

P astor Shane Warren is the lead pastor of The Assembly West Monroe. A prolific author and speaker, he has stirred the church to pursue God's presence more than His presents and cherish His gift of eternal life above any earthly gift.

He took a church that was floundering in 2003 to a gathering place for eagles. The church membership has increased tenfold and a Bible school that trains upward of thirty youth leaders annually is growing by leaps and bounds on the church campus.

Testimonies of restoration, abundance, and deliverance abound in the Assembly. For Pastor Shane Warren, however, it was through the fire and through the storm. As God's set him to the work, Satan challenged him; but he refused to cower or cave in and quit!

There Will Be a Hereafter

At the young age of forty-three, Pastor Shane had a heart attack. His father and grandfather had both died of heart attacks at that age. Just before the attack, Shane's father and grandfather appeared to him in a vision and asked him to go to the hospital if he didn't want to join them just then in eternity.

Pastor Shane persisted though, braving through the chest pain for a week. When he finally went to the hospital, he was catheterized and had a stent placed in an artery that was more than 99 percent blocked.

The following month, he felt dizzy and almost passed out on the platform in front of the congregation. His heart doctor recommended a biventricular pacemaker as a precautionary device, and he underwent the procedure. On the way to operating room, Pastor Shane remembers asking God, "Is this [sickness] going to kill me?"

God told him, quoting Revelation 1:19, that the heart condition would not kill him but thrust him into his hereafter! Since that incident, Pastor Shane's ministry has exploded, and more people have come to Jesus than ever before.

He refused to conform to the world's standard, sick stereotype and became a world changer and an example of a healing life. He is physically and spiritually stronger than he has ever been and is fulfilling God's call to raise up disciples and leaders in the body of Christ.

Life lesson 54: Finishing strong depends on your state of mind, not a burst of energy.

God doesn't give you a taste without a testimony or a view without a victory.

Chapter Fifty-Five

Back in the Dock

And by the hands of the apostles were many signs and wonders
wrought among the people; And of the rest durst no man join
himself to them: but the people magnified them.
—Acts 5:12–13

Steve Hill is best known as the evangelist who preached at the Brownsville Revival in Pensacola, Florida, in the 1990s. During that time, he saw a move of God that drew more than four million people from around the world and saved hundreds of thousands of people.

In 2011, the medical community gave Steve Hill up for dead. He had an aggressive stage IV malignant melanoma that had spread to his bones. After several years of chemotherapy and surgical treatments, Steve had only days to live. He could not remember his wife's name and was not aware of his surroundings.

While on his deathbed, he told his wife, Jeri, to take him off all medications. Doctors and friends advised against it, but Jeri listened to the voice of her husband and the Lord. With his last ounce of strength, Steve Hill prayed a prayer that changed his circumstances.

The Prayer That Changed Everything

In what looked to be his last days on earth, Steve Hill prayed, "Jesus, You have a choice. We're best friends, Lord, and I trust You.

You can either take my life and let me die, which the Bible says is gain, or You can let me live, and I will win another million souls for You."

After this prayer vow, Steve Hill made a supernatural recovery. He still undergoes medical and holistic therapy, but eighteen months later, he is healthier than he was while undergoing chemotherapy. He has gone headlong into adding another million souls to the kingdom by participating in numerous evangelistic and ministry outreaches.

His mandate for a million souls has inspired him to write *Avalanche* a book in which he warns against the scourge of false doctrines in these last days. His memory shattered by cancer medication was renewed, and fulfilled his mandate to warn, wage war, and walk in holiness before his death on March 9th, 2014 at the age of Sixty.

Life lesson 55: Rescue is incomplete without release.

Habit is not holiness, and routine is not righteousness.

Chapter Fifty-Six

Raised from the Dead

Who through faith subdued kingdoms, wrought righteousness, obtained promises, stopped the mouths of lions. Quenched the violence of fire, escaped the edge of the sword, out of weakness were made strong, waxed valiant in fight, turned to flight the armies of the aliens. Women received their dead raised to life again.
—Hebrews 11:33–35

Pastor Daniel Ekechukwu the pastor of Power Chapel Onitsha, Nigeria, was in a horrible car crash in 2000. He suffered massive internal injuries and was unconscious for a day before he died. His wife, being a pastor's wife, thought of nothing but "Women received their dead raised to life" in Hebrews 11:35.

Instead of embalming him and preparing for the funeral, Pastor Ekechukwu's wife took the corpse from the mortuary to a church where Reinhard Bonnke was leading a three day "Fire Conference" for thirty-seven thousand pastors, evangelists, and church leaders.

Pastor Ekechukwu had not breathed for three days and had been certified dead by a medical professional. The cause of death was identified as severe brain damage. His corpse was placed in the basement of the megachurch.

Overcoming Death and Doom

In the upper room where Reinhard Bonnke was preaching, he called for life to return to the body of the corpse. Meanwhile, Pastor

Ekechukwu had been taken to the gates of hell as a result of his vindictive and unforgiving spirit toward his wife.

As the angel of death was about to usher him into hell, he heard Reinhard Bonnke's voice calling him back to life. God then told him to return to earth and warn the people about the dangers of unforgiveness and holding onto past hurts.

In the church basement, meanwhile, Pastor Ekechukwu's corpse drew a deep breath and came back to his physical and mental faculties. He resurrected from the dead after three days because his wife believed Hebrews 11:35.

Today, he goes around the country testifying of the power of God over death and doom. He also warns the church against being partisan, petty, and proud in these last days as Jesus imminent return beckons.

Life lesson 56: We have one life to live, so we should give ours all we have.

Behind the verse is his voice, and behind his voice is your victory.

Chapter Fifty-Seven

From Schizophrenic to Supernatural

Now thanks be unto God, which always causes us to triumph in Christ,
and makes manifest the savor of his knowledge by us in every place.
—2 Corinthians 2:14

G ary Whetstone is the senior pastor of Victory Christian fellowship in Delaware in the United States. A multitalented and gifted pastor and preacher, Gary and his wife, Faye Whetstone, have been pastors for over thirty-five years and have seen God expand their ministry worldwide.

He is the president of Gary Whetstone Worldwide ministries and has developed an online Bible curriculum with video and audio productions that has enabled laypeople in rural communities to obtain degrees in ministry.

He has a doctorate in religious education and has impacted hundreds of thousands of lives with his teachings. It did not, however, start this way. Gary went from being labeled a schizophrenic to what he is today!

Schizophrenic, Stupid, or Supernatural?

In his teenage years, Gary became entangled with drugs, sex, violence, a motorcycle gang, and a destructive lifestyle following a car accident. Worst of all, he became so violent and suicidal that he had to be admitted to a mental health institution.

He was scheduled to undergo an electronic lobotomy of the brain and, as a result, be confined for life with the brain of a three-year-old. One day, however, a voice told him to run, and he ran from the hospital after borrowing shoes and a coat. He was hit by a car driven by one of the clinical psychologists at the hospital.

Instead of immediately calling the police as she would normally have done, she listened to God, who told her, "Do not call the police because he is mine." She told Dr. Whetstone this fifteen years later when she heard his testimony on radio.

Totally Cleaned Up

Whetstone drove to Florida from Delaware. While there, waiting for his fake ID and preparing for life as a fugitive, he prayed, "God, if You are real, I want to go back to Delaware and be given a clean mental health so I can live free and without fear." He immediately received a peace that passed human comprehension, and he drove back to the mental institution.

He asked the hospital to test him with every test they had but not to give him any medications and keep him in the open section of the asylum because he was sane, not insane.

They agreed, and the results astounded them. The findings confirmed Gary's assertion that he was sane; they said he had no clinical reason for ever being termed insane. They originally planned lobotomy for his brain tumor was cancelled because there was no evidence of a tumor on his brain scans.

Gary was discharged and has been preaching the gospel since then. He has been married for almost forty years, has two children and six grandchildren, and has seen countless miracles when he prayed for the sick and infirmed. His life is a testimony of a healing life that went from schizophrenic to supernatural.

Life lesson 57: God does a makeover—spirit, soul, and body—like no one else!

PART VI

Healing Lives—Parishioners

I have a Jewish master—Jesus—and His emoluments are out of this world!

Chapter Fifty-Eight

Melanoma Stopped by
the Power of God

*[Jesus] healed all that were sick that it might be fulfilled which was spoken by
Esaias the prophet, saying, Himself took our infirmities, and bare our sicknesses.*
—Matthew 8:16–17

R. S. (not her real name) is a committed Christian. She has worked and served in the church all her adult life and has seen five generations of her family serve as church leaders in our assembly over the last eighty years.

She had been diagnosed with malignant melanoma in 1999 and underwent radical surgery. She was deemed cancer-free until February 2013, when she noticed a swelling on her right thigh.

The swelling was a swollen pelvic lymph node. It was biopsied and diagnosed as stage IV metastatic melanoma, one of the most aggressive skin cancers.

Thirty Days to Healing

Meanwhile, the church was in prayer for R. S. On a Wednesday night service, the Lord told me as I sat in the congregation that in thirty days R. S. would be healed. I shared that with my wife, and we kept R. S. and her family in our prayers.

R. S.'s surgeon sent her to one of the foremost cancer centers in the world, where doctors removed the large area of the growth along with thirty-seven other lymph nodes.

About thirty days from the day God gave me that word, R. S. returned to her oncologist for follow-up. He said all the lymph nodes biopsied during the surgery were negative, and she had no evidence of further spread of the disease. The doctor did not prescribe chemotherapy or adjunct additional therapy; he simply counseled R. S. to follow up every six months and to monitor the site of surgery for any recurrence. To date, R. S. is living strong and healthy with no trace of a recurrence. Praise God!

Life lesson 58: Follow the Holy Spirit's instruction no matter what.

You can't see the secrets of
God and remain a secret.

Chapter Fifty-Nine

From Anger to Angel

Ye are a chosen generation, a royal priesthood, an holy nation, a
peculiar people that ye should shew forth the praises of him who
hath called you out of darkness into his marvelous light.
—1 Peter 2:9

W hen she was just five months old, A. F. (not her real name) had a traumatic experience. In the car, while waiting for her dad to buy medicine for her sick brother, she fell out from her mother's inadvertent push and broke her legs. The hospital diagnosed her with a fracture that looked like it had been done on purpose and forthwith labeled it child abuse. The hospital called child protective services, and for the next eighteen years, A. F. went from one foster home to another.

She had had cerebral palsy since birth. She always had limited mobility and was unable to walk or stand; she needed a wheelchair for every activity. She became resentful, cynical, and very depressed. She lost self-esteem and attempted on several occasions to kill herself.

However, she gave her life to Jesus when she was eight and under the care of a Christian foster parent, and for a time, she felt the weight lift off her shoulders. She, however, was still angry. She was angry with her parents for crushing her legs and for her being put in multiple foster homes. She was angry with the medical world for "doping" her up on various medications and for leaving her a recluse. Most of all, she was angry with society for her insecure and insignificant feelings about herself.

Desperate and Despised but Delivered

When A. F. came to the health center where I worked, she was very upset. She wanted a document verifying her disability but frowned, growled, and snarled all through our conversation. She countered every smile of mine with an angry retort and left hurriedly with her signed document.

Six months later, I saw A. F. again in my clinic, but this time she was smiling and comforted. Everything seemed to have changed for her overnight. She had been ministered to by a deliverance minister in my community. She had stopped taking her mental health medications, had gotten out of her wheelchair by the power of God, and had gotten reacquainted with her parents thirty-four years after their forced separation.

She became part of a biological family again and even changed her name back to her biological parents' name. She turned her captivity around from being despised to being delivered, from being rejected to being reconciled with God, family, and society.

Every day to her is an opportunity to catch up with time lost. She spends as much time with her biological parents as possible. The outbursts of anger have been replaced by angelic smiles that leave her environment blessed beyond measure.

Life lesson 59: Never, never, give up. Your miracle is on the way.

Safety is not in the absence of danger but in the presence of God.

Chapter Sixty

From HIV/AIDS to Health Allocations!

I shall not die but live and declare the works of the Lord.
—Psalm 118:17

A. N. (not her real name) was ten when she found out she had HIV. She had undergone an open-heart surgery in a tertiary hospital seven years before and had received HIV-infected blood then.

Her life took a nosedive. She became repeatedly ill. Her elementary school stopped her from attending classes for fear of infecting other children, and, worst of all, her church stigmatized her by keeping her separate from other kids in Sunday school.

There was, however, one ray of light in her life. Her mother, an ardent believer and prayer warrior, refused to give up on her. She took her from one research hospital to the other in pursuit of a cure for this malady that was at the time considered a death sentence.

On a particular occasion, when it looked as if every possible hope was lost and A. N. was not going to survive, she cried out to God, reminding Him of Deuteronomy 7:15: "And the Lord will take away from thee all sickness, and will put none of the evil diseases of Egypt, which thou knowest, upon thee."

Thirty Years Later

Defying all the odds stacked against her by science, society, and Satan, A. N. lived. She gave her life to Jesus and asked God to make her a vessel to honor that people would use to testify of the goodness of God.

Twenty years after her inadvertent infection and ten years after her diagnosis, A. N. was just happy to be alive. She never imagined any man would want to marry her and thought she would be a childless spinster.

She was wrong. She met a Christian gentleman who loved her and wanted to marry her. When A. N. told him she was HIV positive, he said, "God knew what you had before I asked to marry you, and God will preserve me."

Today, they are the proud parents of two lovely children. Against all medical odds, her husband and children are HIV-negative and in perfect health. They live in the suburbs of West Monroe, Louisiana, and are active witnesses for Jesus.

A. N. has shared her testimony on television, at pulpits, and in one-on-one interactions. She believes God gave her another opportunity at life to glorify Him. She takes her antiretroviral medicine daily but confesses to any who would listen that she is healed and expects a full manifestation in God's good time.

The medical community has tried to put her in a box, but A. N. has refused to live there. Before she married, doctors asked to perform an elective hysterectomy because they feared the repercussions of pregnancy on her already fragile body.

She refused and has successfully undergone two, full-term vaginal deliveries without complications. They attempted to stop her being a mother and a wife, but God's will prevailed. Today, she knows that everything God has purposed for her is attainable, and she refuses to be stopped until they are fully accomplished.

Life lesson 60: What God does for one, He will do for all who believe in Jesus.

God will never send you where He cannot sustain you, and He will never keep you doing what you are not keen about.

Chapter Sixty-One

Prostate Cancer Pulverized

Through desire a man, having separated himself,
seeketh and intermeddleth with all wisdom.
—Proverbs 18:1

A t one of our Holy Ghost Night meetings in Monroe, Louisiana, the Word of the Lord came to me about M. S. (not her real name). God told me there was a healing He wanted to carry out on her father.

I asked generally if anyone in the room needed prayer for a father, but no one responded. After a few moments, the Holy Spirit impressed me again the need to pray for this M. S.'s father, and I called her out and told her what God had told me.

In response, she told me that her father had died but that her husband had recently been diagnosed with prostate cancer and was undergoing treatment at a cancer institute. He had almost died during one of the sessions, but she had seen God's hand confirming his healing by this particular Word of knowledge

She testified that she had not mentioned the condition to anyone outside her family and that only God could have revealed it to me. At that moment, I realized that Sarah "obeyed Abraham, calling him lord (*or meaning father*)" (1 Peter 3:6). God was healing this man because of his wife's obedience to God!

Desire, Dedication, and Devotion

M. S. first met me as her mother's doctor. Apart from being excited about God at every turn and updating me with scintillating testimonies of God's active providence in her and her family, she always carried a Christian book to read while waiting for me.

In a culture that is slowly becoming illiterate and a congregation that avoids responsibility but wants rewards, M. S. was a breath of fresh air. She inspired me from the books she read and asked me to agree with her for even more miracles.

Her husband finished his cancer treatment, and she now believes he is cancer-free. He tells M. S. to keep on praying as he has seen the effects of her prayers on his health and family.

Today, M. S. ministers in prisons, at women's conferences, and in Vacation Bible Schools because of her deep desire for God that has birthed a dedication and devotion to God that is clear for all to see.

Life lesson 61: One moment of power can change a lifetime of pain.

Until God breaks you, you remain breakable in the hands of men.

Chapter Sixty-Two

Chronic Lower Back Pain Disappears

These signs shall follow them that believe; In my name shall they
cast out devils; they shall speak with new tongues; They shall take
up serpents and if they drink any deadly thing, it shall not hurt
them. They shall lay hands on the sick, and they shall recover.
—Mark 16:17–18

R. B. (not his real name) had been my patient for about a year. He had multiple health and social problems. On each visit, he was accompanied by his lovely wife, and he kept me updated on the latest twists in the tales of his life. One tale he never failed to relate was how much his lower back hurt.

His medical history was lengthy, and he had undergone multiple spinal interventions, invasive and noninvasive, without improvement. On the social side, I was enamored at the love between R. B. and his wife. They had been married for forty-six years, had seven children, and were determined to get through his health concerns together.

He was attending another church when I met him and had a burning desire for more of God. He started attending my church in West Monroe, Louisiana, and quickly "plugged in." While R. B. became an ardent Sunday school attendee, his wife became a member of the choir. The lower back pain, however, still persisted.

Healing in His Wings

At a church meeting hosted by an evangelist from Cleveland, Tennessee, R. B. came forward for prayer. The man of God laid hands on him, and at the end of the service, R. B. told me he was healed. His long-standing chronic lower back pain had gone. He had no more exercise restrictions, and he was pain-free. He was so excited at his healing, and soon afterward, his whole family was attending the church.

One moment in the presence of God is worth more than thousands spent elsewhere. R. B. knows this. No wonder that when the doors open for church, R. B. is always there. Praise God.

Life lesson 62: What God's singular touch can do, man's multiple touches cannot.

When you stand on the Word of God for your miracle after having done all to stand, you won't have to stand for your miracle very long.

Chapter Sixty-Three

Third Time Triumphant

*Ye shall serve the L*ORD *your God, and he shall bless thy bread, and thy water and take sickness away from the midst of thee. There shall nothing cast their young, nor be barren, in thy land and the number of thy days He (God) will fulfill.*
—Exodus 23:25–26

R. Q. (not her real name) and her husband were new to our church. In my meet-and-greet conversation with them, they told me how they had lost two pregnancies in the space of one year. R. Q. had had two successful pregnancies but desperately wanted a third. According to her physicians, she seemed unable to carry another fetus to term.

These dedicated Christians rededicated themselves to serving the Lord. She joined the choir, and her husband began transporting members to church with the church bus.

Within three months, I saw both of them in my clinic beaming with smiles—R. Q. was pregnant. This time though, she knew her kingdom rights as a child of God and stood on Exodus 23:26: "None shall cast their young or be barren."

Breaking the Stronghold of Fear

R. Q. refused to remain afraid this time. When the Devil made suggestions of a miscarriage or a preterm end of her pregnancy, she spoke the Word of God back to that thought and prevailed.

In the midst of her pregnancy, there were times she would seemingly lose control of her emotions and become extremely panicky and fearful. Her family and the church, however, rallied around her and prayed the prayer of faith over her, and she was delivered.

At forty weeks, the beautiful baby girl R. Q. and her husband had waited for so long was born. The baby and her mother came through triumphant the third time! If we stand on God's Word notwithstanding hell's fury, His Word will ultimately prevail.

Life lesson 63: When fear knocks on the door of your heart, send faith to answer and fear will disappear.

*It is not over until God
says, "It's over."*

Chapter Sixty-Four

Breast Cancer Busted

He cast out the spirits with his word, and healed all that were sick
that it might be fulfilled which was spoken by Esaias the prophet,
saying, Himself took our infirmities, and bare our sicknesses.
—Matthew 8:16–17

U. M. (not her real name) was diagnosed with metastatic breast cancer in 2011. She was a faithful member of our church, and prayer and supplication was going up daily for her and her family.

She underwent extensive surgery on her left breast and began chemotherapy and hormonal therapy after that.

Through it all, U. M. was positive; she was always speaking the Word of God and confessing the Scriptures at every turn. She told the Lord before the treatment began, "Lord, this is not about me—It is all about You."

Three Years Later

U. M. recovered from the treatment and returned to her profession and ministry. She sings in the choir, is a member of the church prayer team, and serves as a teacher for special-needs children.

On one Sunday morning, God gave a word of prophecy, saying He was going to heal a "Minnie" completely and raise her up out of sickness. She approached me after service and said "Mimmi" was her pet name. She believed the word was for her, especially since she was preparing to follow up with her cancer physician soon. We prayed together and believed God to fulfill the inspired prophecy.

At the last examination U. M. has been certified completely recovered of cancer with no evident trace left in her body. She stood in faith, fought the good fight, and won the battle. Praise God!

Life lesson 64: Nothing stops Satan like faith.

It is not whom you tussle with that matters but whom you trust.

Chapter Sixty-Five

Anxiety Annihilated

*And the peace of God, which passeth all understanding, shall
keep your hearts and minds through Christ Jesus.*
—Philippians 4:7

T. A. (not his real name) was working and attending college simultaneously. He was an engineering major and on the school basketball at a prestigious Southern college. He looked like the ideal role model for young African Americans his age.

His dad was coming regularly to the monthly Holy Ghost Night services my wife and I were conducting. After a Sunday morning church service, T. A.'s dad took me aside and poured out his heart about his son's worsening anxiety and exacerbating paranoia.

Apparently, T. A. was so afraid to go out that it was negatively affecting his secular, school, and social life. He was so afraid that he would cry like a baby if someone challenged him to confront those fears. He couldn't go out alone or stand in front of people to speak.

T. A.'s dad was obviously very concerned. I asked him to bring T. A. to one of our night meetings for a supernatural encounter.

Taking Healing by Force

At the meeting, the brethren were encouraged to resist the Devil and watch him flee. We took authority over bondages of fear, anxiety, and panic in brethrens' lives and spoke a prophetic word over them.

Toward the end of our five-hour prayer meeting, I asked for anyone who wanted special prayers to come forward. T. A. stepped forward. I could see desire well up in him to be free again. He wanted to be free, and even though he knew he had to be at work in three hours, he had come, expecting the miraculous. We surrounded T. A., laid hands on him, anointed him with oil, cast out any evil, demonic plantings in him, and decreed him free forever.

To this day, T. A has walked in boldness, fears no evil anymore, is in a budding relationship with a Christian girl, and is a top-tier employee at his company.

Life lesson 65: Turnarounds and breakthroughs are God's specialty.

Prayer is not just talking but knowing to whom you are talking.

Chapter Sixty-Six

Colon Cancer Crushed

Jesus answered and said, Every plant, which my heavenly
Father hath not planted, shall be rooted up.
—Matthew 15:13

R. A. (not her real name) worked as a registered nurse in Monroe, Louisiana. She's in her midfifties and has had a deep, personal walk with God since she was a teenager.

She felt some abdominal pain and started taking some gastric reflux medications; she kept that up for three months, but the abdominal pain worsened. She then went in for diagnosis, and investigations showed a mass-like structure in her colon that may have invaded the surrounding tissue.

The surgeon immediately scheduled her for exploratory surgery with the possibility of chemotherapy and radiation therapy if the tumor was invasive. R. A. conceded but asked for time to make one more prayer to the father.

I Am Not Ready, Lord!

R. A. was scheduled for surgery to cut out the mass the next day. All alone in her room, she cried out to God, asking for His supernatural manifestation of healing in her body.

She explained to God that she was not afraid to die but that she would appreciate more time on earth to fulfill her destiny. God reassured her of His healing power, and that night, she dreamed of a man in white clothing operating on her and closing her up again.

The next day, she went into surgery. The surgeon, convinced she had invasive cancer of the colon, excised a large part of her colon and adjoining lymph nodes. He asked her to follow up with him in three days.

Three days later, the surgeon saw R. A. in his office and was bewildered. She did not have a trace of cancer among what he had excised or in the multiple lymph nodes removed. The surgeon kept muttering idly to himself, "There must be a mistake," but there was incontrovertible evidence that R. A. was cancer-free.

To date, R. A. is still cancer-free. She takes every moment as extra time from God to finish the work He gave her and to leave a mark on eternity. The Master Surgeon removed the cancer in her by crushing colon cancer!

Life lesson 66: Dying ashamed may get you into heaven, but it will stop you living a life of destiny.

Faith makes all things possible—not easy.

Chapter Sixty-Seven

Called, Set Apart, and Delivered

Moreover whom he did predestinate, them he also called: and whom he called,
them he also justified: and whom he justified, them he also glorified.
—Romans 8:30

J. K. (not her real name) and her husband were the closest family to us when we arrived in Monroe, Louisiana. Her husband introduced me to the prison ministry and was instrumental in many ministry opportunities in the church and overseas.

She was in her early forties when she developed a mass on the left side of her neck. It was soft, nontender, and rapidly increasing in size. She went in to see if it could be drained. The results were inconclusive. Her doctors advised her to take some medications to regulate her metabolism and to keep an eye on it to see if it continued growing. She turned the medical malady over to God. Anointed men of God anointed her with oil, and prayers were made for her healing.

No Weapon Shall Prosper

It was while praying on one occasion that J. K. had a revelation that the swelling of her jaw was a spiritual, not a physical attack. She took authority over it and called forth her healing.

It took nearly one year, but eventually, the swelling went away. Her experience made J. K. throw caution to the winds and become more audacious in her quest for God. She understood her authority as a believer more and decided to exercise it!

She saw her experience as an opportunity for spiritual growth and furthering her ministry to people with such illnesses. Today, she is considered a pillar in the house of God. A reliable stalwart for the faith, she has seen her faith go from strength to strength, from glory to glory, and from faith to faith.

Life lesson 67: Become too expensive for the Devil to mess with by walking in faith that never quits.

You get your miracle not by coincidence or convenience but by confidence in God.

Chapter Sixty-Eight

Finishing Strong

Unto you that fear my name shall the Sun of righteousness arise with healing
in his wings; and ye shall go forth, and grow up as calves of the stall.
—Malachi 4:2

D. W. (not his real name) is a wealthy man in Louisiana who
has sown tremendous amounts of money into the kingdom of
God. Sometime in 2004, he found a knot in his leg which was
diagnosed stage IV lymphoma, a rare cancer that is difficult to treat.

He went to the best cancer treatment centers in the country and
was told by specialists he had three months to live. They advised him
to undergo palliative chemotherapy and major bowel surgery for the
condition.

He underwent chemotherapy but did not undergo exploratory
surgery because the medical experts opined that, even if he had the
best possible care, he would not live more than a year.

At the time, D. W. was in his fifties and not ready to die. His fledgling
construction business was not at the point he wanted, his wife needed
him, and his children were doing their own thing outside the will of
God and he wanted to see them restored in the faith. He took his case
to God, and the supernatural God exploded everything around him!

Supernatural Increase in Ten Years

D. W. went from stage IV carcinoma to totally healed. The same doctors who told him he would die in three months acknowledged ten years later that D. W. was healthier than anyone else his age and that without a doubt the cancer was gone.

Ten years after the initial diagnosis, D. W. felt a mass in his groin. He asked me and some other Christians to pray for him and went for a biopsy of the mass.

In between the prayer and the biopsy of the mass, God gave a word to D. W. that healing was in His wings and not on man's wings or abilities (Malachi 4:2). He recognized then that he had taken responsibility for his health instead of letting God be God through him. He repented and underwent the biopsy of the mass.

The biopsy came back negative for cancer. Meanwhile, everything D. W. had delved into had prospered. His business went on a perpetual upswing, even in the midst of a recession, and his family was restored back to kingdom servants for the Lord.

His personal spiritual walk is fervent and has recently welcomed a third generation with the birth of his grandchildren. He is now in his midsixties and is confidently finishing strong!

Life lesson 68: God is more interested in the evidence than the explanation and in the results than the reports.

Our life is His business;
His business is our life.

Chapter Sixty-Nine

Deliverance by Decree

Is any sick among you? Let him call for the elders of the church and let them pray over him, anointing him with oil in the name of the Lord and the prayer of faith shall save the sick, and the Lord shall raise him up.
—James 5:14–15

A. S. (not her real name) and her husband had been the first couple my wife and I met when we joined the Assembly West Monroe. As leaders of the young couples' class, they quickly warmed up to us. Soon, we involved ourselves with their class and with a host of other activities.

Apparently, they were famous for their softball and T-ball exploits with their kids. We were soon traveling with them, visiting towns and watching interstate championships with their family.

Since A. S. is an astonishingly active woman and former athlete, I was surprised when she asked me to pray for her one Sunday while I was ministering to others. She was crying, and her husband was right behind her. A. S. asked for divine healing of a jaw mass that had suddenly appeared in the previous three days.

Supernatural Solution

I laid hands on A. S., anointed her with oil according to James 5:14, and decreed that the swelling disappear. Apparently, there were concerns and challenges about the possibility of cancer. I commanded

212

the uprooting of the mass according to Matthew 15:13 and commanded healing on A. S.'s body.

The following week, I received a praise report that after the prayer, the jaw mass had shriveled. At the time of the testimony, which was about a week later, the mass had totally disappeared!

A. S. was excited, and we rejoiced in her healing. She has since returned to the T-ball and softball circuit and is, as usual, full of activities. She is tumor-free to date. Hallelujah!

Life lesson 69: One word from God is more powerful than many words from others.

God does not need a millennium to change your situation; He needs only a moment.

Chapter Seventy

The Boy Born Blind

*Who his own self bare our sins in his own body on the tree, that we, being dead
to sins, should live unto righteousness [and] by whose stripes ye were healed.*
—1 Peter 2:24

I joined the Assembly West Monroe as a parishioner in July 2010. As long as I could remember, the grandfather of T. U. (not his real name) had been a regular feature at the prayer altars and during any time of healing ministrations.

When T. U. was a newborn, his parents were told he would never see, would never defecate normally, and would be forever mentally challenged. His parents, too consumed by sorrow because of T. U's condition, considered him an invalid who would never be able to fully actualize normal human potential. They kept him at his grandfather's home, and his being there was the beginning of the miraculous in T. U.'s life.

One Moment of Prayer

One day, T. U. was walking about in church with a guide rod. Rita, my wife, was stirred at this sight, and she asked T. U.'s grandfather if she could pray for him. He agreed.

After pouring out her heart to God, she released T. U. to his grandfather, expecting a miracle. At the next service, T. U.'s grandfather

215

came up to the pulpit and, even before the sermon could commence, started giving T. U.'s testimony.

Apparently, it was considered impossible for T. U. to defecate due to an anus that hadn't developed as it should have, but he said that T. U. had moved his bowels three times in the last twenty-four hours. He considered this an indicator of God's healing power at work, and the church claimed the other healing benefits for T. U.

Life lesson 70: Persistence will break down the most impervious of situations.

Born in the fire,
I could not be content in smoke
—Mae Taylor Roberts (from an essay
in 1932 *Pentecostal Evangel*)

Chapter Seventy-One

Expectation: The Catalyst for Miracles

And he gave heed unto them, expecting to receive something of them. Then Peter said, Silver and gold have I none; but such as I have give I thee: In the name of Jesus Christ of Nazareth rise up and walk. And he took him by the right hand, and lifted him up: and immediately his feet and ankle bones received strength.
—Acts 3:5–7

E. D. (not his real name) hurt his back on a mission trip to Latin America. Even when he returned to the United States, he still faced severe debilitating lower back pain.

He had gone to several spine surgeons and had tried multiple physical and pharmacological therapies, but he was still no better. Hungry and desperate for a miracle, He came to one of our Sunday school meetings. He wanted to be free from narcotics and the state of stupor they left him in.

That day, I taught about the fear of God and about how walking in man's fear stops the sovereignty of God from working in our lives. He sat there, expectantly receiving every word, and as he did so, God did not disappoint.

Healed, Restored, and Delivered

E. D. went home healed that day, and the next day at a midweek church prayer meeting, he shared his testimony. He said he had stood up from that Sunday school meeting stronger than he had ever stood and with the least amount of pain. He was able to lift things and do chores he had formerly been unable to do. He felt more pain-free than ever.

Most of all, he experienced a liberty of the spirit he had never before experienced. He came to church expectant and had walked away healed, restored, and delivered!

Life lesson 71: What God does for one, He will readily do for all if they all believe.

God is coming for a glorious church, not a garbage church.

Chapter Seventy-Two

The Matchless God

But when Jesus heard it [the death of Jairus's daughter], he answered Jairus, saying Fear not: believe only, and she shall be made whole.
—Luke 8:50

T. S. (not her real name) was in her midseventies. She sat down in the congregation and listened to every word I spoke as I taught Sunday school. I was teaching about how with human beings some things are impossible, with God, all things are possible.

She listened with rapt attention. She wanted a miracle beyond what humanity or medications could provide. Unbeknownst to me, T. S. was being tormented daily with chronic sinusitis. She found it difficult to breathe and had even fainted once while touring a mountain in Jerusalem. She was forced to limit outdoor activities because of this malady.

Her condition had become so bad that her husband began considering where to bury her! As she listened to me, as I preached out of Luke 8:50, she decided it was faith without fear or a lifetime of breathlessness. She chose the former!

Polyps Are Coming Out of My Nose!
T. S. left that Sunday school class determined to receive her miracle. Having prayed and believed, T. S. and her husband stood on the Word of God for her healing. As a result, something extraordinary

started happening. Brownish-grey sediments began coming out of T. S.'s nostrils, and no one could explain it. She was breathing better by the day, and she brought those sediments to me, saying she had not felt that good in years.

The next week, in unabated excitement, she and her husband told us the entire story of her healing. A. S. had broken in one hour what had taken a lifetime to evolve. She took the polyps she had discharged from her nostrils to her specialist physicians, and they told her it was inexplicable.

God had given her a testimony of healing that forever changed her life. It was beyond human comprehension but well within divine realization.

Life lesson 72: Everything is probable, not just possible, when God gets involved.

You will either fear God alone or fear someone or something less than God.

Chapter Seventy-Three

Delivered from Fear

God hath not given us the spirit of fear; but of power,
and of love, and of a sound mind.
—2 Timothy 1:7

T. M. (not her real name) came to our city from Mississippi for a master's degree program. She joined our church and became actively involved in small groups and young students' meetings.

On a particular Monday, I received a call from the pastor asking me to check on T. M. She was having difficulty swallowing and had been to several hospitals, emergency rooms, and clinics without resolution.

I asked her to come to my clinic for further investigation. When her laboratory and radiological tests returned negative for any diseases, I told her she had a psychosomatic condition called pseudodysphagia and recommended some antidepressants and antianxiety medications.

I Want to Blow My Head Off!

She did not improve; she became worse. She came under ungodly torment and was at a time so afraid she could not drive from her small group leader's place to her house thirty minutes away out of fear!

She lost self-confidence and spent hours on end crying. She began to contemplate suicide and decided she was going to end her life with a gunshot. She chose a shop to buy ammunition but decided to stop at her school library to drop her borrowed school materials first.

T. M. had been called out at the midweek prayer service days before for deliverance. Those prayers started a chain reaction that eventually led to the breaking of the spirit of intimidation, inferiority, and insecurity that had taken over her life.

The school library manager where T. M. went spent two hours with her, chronicling her own personal challenges with depression. She shared about her own ill-fated suicide attempt; she had decided to drive off a cliff, but God had locked her car doors so she could not perform her act of doom.

The special attention the office manager had given T. M. coupled with the prayers of the saints days before set her free. She saw her life as valuable to God, not something to be ended by suicide.

Today, she is free from fear and has no plans to end her life. She is near completion of her master's thesis, is walking in the liberty of the Holy Spirit, and is manifesting the Spirit of love, power, and a sound mind. Hallelujah!

Life lesson 73: Give God your lifetime, and He will give you life eternal.

God does not want reasoning;
He wants repentance.

Chapter Seventy-Four

Cervical Cancer Cut Out

And a woman having an issue of blood twelve years, which had spent all her
living upon physicians, neither could be healed of any, came behind him, and
touched the border of his garment: and immediately her issue of blood stanched.
—Luke 8:43–44

R. U. (not her real name) is the leader of the women's group in the church and a virtuous daughter of God. When she was diagnosed with metastatic cancer of the cervix, she was in stupor and shock.

She came to church but didn't tell anyone about her diagnosis; she trusted God to speak to her about her situation. Having a son survive cancer boosted her faith, but she wanted a word for her situation that day.

I got up that Sunday morning and delivered a word I had received from the Lord to the congregation stating that the worst was over and that His best would soon manifest. Afterward, R. U. and her husband besieged me. They told me the word I spoke was precisely the word they needed, and we prayed together.

Saved, Healed, and Delivered

Two months later, R. U. went under a doctor's knife and had a hysterectomy. They scanned her postoperatively and told her that though her cancer was of an aggressive sort, it had not spread beyond the womb.

She recovered fully from the surgery and once again worked in her ministry of leading women into the presence of God. She believes every moment she lives is a privilege and must be fully maximized.

Ten years ago, her son had suffered with an aggressive tumor of the kidney and made a full recovery. She has seen God's hand in action through both cases and wants the world to know about His saving love.

Life lesson 74: God does not follow protocol; He follows altar calls.

Whom you serve in life will determine what life serves you.

Chapter Seventy-Five

God of Supernatural Increase

The Lord shall increase you more and more, you and your children.
—Psalm 115:14

V. K. (not his real name) was in his midforties and had suffered with HIV/AIDS for more than a decade. He started coming to the Assembly West Monroe, Louisiana, with his parents but did not fully acknowledge Jesus as Lord and Savior. His parents took him before God in prayer, but V. K. seemed to deteriorate spiritually and physically.

One day, he just walked out of the house, leaving a note that told his mother not to bother looking for him as he had to take care of some business. The mother suspected he had returned to a past drug habit and in desperation asked us to pray for his recovery and restoration.

V. K.'s parents were not troubled in spite of not knowing his whereabouts. They handed him over to God in faith and vowed to leave him there. Prayer was made in confidence to God, knowing He alone could ordain recovery and restoration of even the most wayward sinner.

Go Home and Die

When V. K. reappeared three months later, he was critically sick. His weight had dropped to about seventy-five pounds, and he was rushed to the hospital. The attending physician treating him advised the parents to take him home to die.

The parents did not obey the doctor's orders; they took V. K. and his medical problems to God in prayer. Less than twenty-four hours after the prayers began, V. K. improved markedly.

The following ninety days saw V. K. continue to improve. His weight went from 75 pounds to 145 pounds in less than two months. The doctor who counseled V. K. to go home and die was shocked when next he saw him.

God not only healed V. K. physically but also gave him a new beginning spiritually through Jesus Christ. He rededicated his life to Jesus Christ, stopped abusing alcohol and drugs, and is currently on antiretroviral medications. He continues to attend Sunday school and church faithfully and has recently joined the church choir.

V. K. did not die simply because his parents believed God could do what he said in His Word, and a church family agreed with her in prayer. Glory to God!

Life lesson 75: When men come to their end, God starts.

To be lionhearted, you
must first invite the lion
of the tribe of Judah in.

Chapter Seventy-Six

Called to Peace, Not Pieces

Say to them that are of a fearful heart, Be strong, fear not: behold, your God will come with vengeance, even God with a recompense; he will come and save you.
—Isaiah 35:4

A droit and alert, R. U. (not her real name) walked up to me after she heard me preach about the tragedy of giving heed to the spirit of fear; she wanted to be free of that spirit.

I bent toward her, ready to pray a prayer of agreement with her, when the Holy Spirit told me to ask her to forgive her sister. He said that until she forgave her sister, she would remain in bondage to fear!

As I declared this revelation to R. U., she started sobbing. She explained to me the debacle she and her sister's relationship had become. She wanted her sister to apologize to her first, then she would then apologize.

After further counseling and the application of the Word of God by R. U., she unconditionally came to love her sister. She uprooted any roots of bitterness and strife in her life toward her sister and, through prayer and love, fear finally was dealt a deathblow in her life.

Tears of Joy

R. U. forgave her sister and asked God for His healing balm on her heart. The family that had been strewn with strife and shame harvested deliverance and destiny from God.

When R. U. forgave her sister, she walked free from fear. She has no more panic attacks and is fearless in life and ministry. She smiles effortlessly and finds it easier to socialize with others.

By one decision, R. U. changed her life. She forgave her sister, and deliverance was the result. She is no more crying tears of unfounded fears but tears of hope, joy, and faith.

Life lesson 76: When you forgive others, God will forgive you.

*Fertility depends on your
fear of God and barrenness
on whom you believe.*

Chapter Seventy-Seven

Miracle Baby

He [God] maketh the barren woman to keep house,
and to be a joyful mother of children.
—Psalm 113:19

J. J. (not her real name) was a successful career woman. Our families had grown close and shared exciting times together. She was a teacher, and her husband was a successful entrepreneur.

J. J. and her husband had been married for four years but had not had any children. These childhood sweethearts had taken their nephews and nieces as their children and continued waiting for God's perfect time.

One day after Sunday morning service, J. J. shared with my wife and me her determination to be a mother. She said that God had given her a love for children and that He would not leave her without someone on whom to pour her motherly affection. She intimated to us that she had decided to undergo in vitro fertilization (IVF) in the hope of realizing God's divine will for her life. We prayed with her. One year later, she had a daughter!

In God's Virtual Future (IVF)

The surgeon treating J. J. was well known for his brash, abrasive style. He was the foremost reproductive endocrinologist in the area, but most Christian women who visited him felt he was overly negative.

Two to four weeks after J. J. had her IVF procedure, she returned to the surgeon for follow-up. He explained to her that the implanted tissue in her womb was nonviable on the basis of her blood tests. He asked J. J. to prepare for an inevitable abortion.

J. J. and her husband were crestfallen, but they refused to believe the doctor's report. They believed God could give life to the implanted tissue in her womb, and they called for prayers from members of the church.

In less than twenty-four hours, the blood tests used to determine the viability of the implanted tissue in J. J.'s womb changed dramatically. When she represented for the elective termination, the surgeon had to swallow his words and state that the fetus was now miraculously alive and fully viable.

J. J. gave birth to a beautiful baby girl nine months later, and her daughter is thriving. None of these miracles would have happened if she had simply accepted fate instead of walking in faith to God's Word!

Life lesson 77: One word from God can change everything.

*He is no fool who gives
what he cannot keep
to gain what he cannot lose.*
—Jim Elliot, martyred missionary
to Ecuador (1927–1956)

Chapter Seventy-Eight

Stroke Sidelined

They brought to him a man sick of the palsy, lying on a bed and Jesus seeing their faith said unto the sick of the palsy; Son, be of good cheer; thy sins be forgiven thee.
—Matthew 9:2

T. H. (not his real name) had been a business executive with all the trappings of power, prestige, and prosperity. He drove the best cars, had the best girls, and lived in the best houses.

He had no time for God. In 2001, however, his world turned upside down. His father died and, while attempting to handle his parents' estate, he suffered a stroke. As a result, he couldn't continue his swashbuckling, razzamatazz lifestyle. He had no sensation in his feet and was unable to maintain his equilibrium.

The left side of his body was weaker than the right side, and physical and medical therapy were not yielding dividends. Finding no solution in the world, T. H. turned to God in desperation and started coming to church.

Miracle in the House

First of all, God gave him a committed Christian lady for a wife, and he began to voraciously feed on the Word of God. To his new wife's dismay, T. H. had not even heard of the story of Moses and the Ten Commandments.

In our Holy Ghost Night meetings and during several church services, T. H. would fall down under the power of the Holy Spirit for hours. When he would rise, his feet would feel better and his balance was better as well.

He became able to walk backward without falling over, and he was steadier than he had been before the power of God came on him. Today, his numbness has disappeared, and he has excellent feeling in both feet.

He has also regained strength in the left side of the body and has begun ministering to the homeless and drug addicts. He has started a care group for hurting people and has established a men's group in his home that supports missions and ministry.

God turned his captivity around because he came home. God will do likewise and more for you when you turn your life over to Him.

Life lesson 78: It is not hard living for Jesus—it is hard living on the fence.

If your memories are bigger
than your dreams,
you are living in the past,
and the past cannot
see the future.
—Dr. Jesse Duplantis

Chapter Seventy-Nine

Fever Set on Fire

And when Jesus was come into Peter's house, he saw his wife's
mother laid, and sick of a fever. And he touched her hand, and the
fever left her: and she arose, and ministered unto them.
—Matthew 8:14–15

A t the Assembly West Monroe in Louisiana, every service is considered a miracle service. At the end of one of our Sunday services, I was accosted by Minister T. H. (not his real name) to come and pray for his wife.

He has been an ardent supporter of our ministry. I was more than delighted to pray for his wife. He led me to a corner of the church parking lot, and I saw his wife shivering and gritting her teeth.

T. H. stood by me as we prayed for his wife. I anointed her with oil and spoke the Word of God over her just as Jesus had with Peter's mother.

It Came to Pass

The following Wednesday, when I saw T. H., he told me that after our prayer for his wife, she went home and was fully recovered for work the next day. All this happened without recourse to medications, hospital emergency room visits, or alternative therapy. Her fever broke immediately after the prayer, and she never missed a day of work.

T. H. continues to minister regularly at our Holy Ghost Nights. Their children and business have blossomed. They, like Peter's mother-in-law, have continued to minister to the saints.

Life lesson 79: Where service to God starts, sickness departs.

There are two kinds of people in the world—opposition thinkers and opportunity takers.

Chapter Eighty

From Drunk Skunk to Dragnet for Souls

They that be wise shall shine as the brightness of the firmament and they that turn many to righteousness as the stars for ever and ever.
—Daniel 12:3

In one Wednesday service at the Assembly West Monroe, R. D. (not his real name) came to the altar a drunk and left delivered from alcoholism. He dropped his bottle of alcohol at the altar and walked away from a bondage that had ravaged him for years.

R. D. was brought up in church, had attended church all his life, and at one point was even a youth minister. In his early years of ministry, however, his wife left him, and he turned against God.

He fell away from church and gave full attention to alcohol. He remarried and had another son, but he never regained the same intimacy with God. He used alcohol as the arbiter of his troubled spirit. In the process, he drifted farther from God.

He, however, had a praying father and mother who never stopped interceding for him. One evening, at a sparsely attended midweek service, the snare was broken, and R. D.'s soul "escaped as a bird out of the snare of the fowlers" (Psalm 124:7).

From Thuggery to Total Transformation

R. D.'s transformation was total. He started a ministry in the local assembly that targeted those with nothing. He organized feeding for the hungry and clothes for the naked, and he took in the homeless and highlighted the plight of the needy to a church that had placed the cause of the poor on the back burner.

His resoluteness and resilience saw to the purchase of a trailer specially equipped to carry tons of food to feed the hungry. His passion for Christ spurred others, including his son, and they march assuredly into their destiny.

He has been alcohol-free since that day in 2011, and he has brought in fellow wayfarers in life into the canopy of heaven by witnessing to them at their place and position. He is so passionate about his alcohol-free life that he even rejects cakes baked with even a whiff of alcohol.

His life is a testimony to the power of God to take a life from the guttermost to the uttermost places of life. In Hebrews 7:25, we read, "God is able to save them to the uttermost that come unto God by Him [Jesus], seeing He ever lives to make intercession for them."

Life lesson 80: If God can use the stones to praise Him, He can certainly use you.

What you bow to obtain will burn to ashes, but what you obey God to obtain will become an asset.

Chapter Eighty-One

Angry and Afraid, or Soft and Supple

*The Spirit of the Lord God is upon me; because the Lord hath anointed
me to preach good tidings unto the meek; he hath sent me to bind up the
brokenhearted... to comfort all that mourn [and] appoint unto them that mourn
in Zion... beauty for ashes, the oil of joy for mourning, the garment of praise
for the spirit of heaviness that they might be called trees of righteousness.*
—Isaiah 61:1–3

A. R. (not her real name) was angry and devastated. She had just lost her dearly beloved baby after six weeks of pregnancy to an ill-fated miscarriage. The event was like a bolt out of the blue and not what A. R. and her husband had expected months after marrying.

They were committed Christians and wondered why this had happened to them. It went against a Christian woman's promise of not prematurely casting her young. Since the baby's death happened so soon after A. R.'s father's death, her mind was in turmoil.

She inadvertently took her grief and anger out on her new husband. She was afraid of losing another child and refused his overtures at intimacy for months. He recoiled into his shell but intensely prayed for her healing.

Healed, Healthy, and Hearty again

One day, God spoke to A. R., and everything changed. He told her to stop being dark, dreadful, and moody and to show love to her husband by intimacy. God's word to A. R. broke her yoke of depression and heaviness. Soon thereafter, in an intimate moment with her spouse, she conceived. She gave birth to a healthy baby girl nine months later.

A. R. has learned to trust God and not tussle with her myriad of problems all alone. She found emotional healing in prayer and the Word of God and lives life heartily again.

A. R. and her husband have since pioneered a healing resort for recovering drug addicts who need reintegration into society. She has learned to become a solution to the problem by being wholly healed of hurts through God's Word.

Life lesson 81: God is tested, tried, and true; He cannot lie.

A closed mouth is
a closed destiny.
—Dr. D. K. Olukoya, general overseer,
Mountain of Fire and Miracles Ministries

Chapter Eighty-Two

Malignant, Misdiagnosed, but with a Miraculous End

We know that all things work together for good to them that love
God, to them who are the called according to his purpose.
—Romans 8:28

E. B. (not her real name) is a spiritual investor in our area. She has sown multiple seeds that have grown into many ministries and has mentored many young women into womanhood by her selfless acts of kindness and compassion.

In 2010, she noticed a rash on her face that was unlike anything she had seen before. It was reddish and rapidly spreading. Her family physician treated her for acne for nearly a year without resolution and then decided to refer her to a surgeon for a biopsy.

When she arrived at the surgeon's office, unbeknownst to her, she saw the wrong surgeon. Apparently, she had gotten the names of the surgeons mixed up and was in the room of another surgeon.

Unaware of her mistake, she saw him, and he took a skin biopsy that revealed a rare but malignant skin cancer called Bowen's disease. This surgeon E. B. had "inadvertently" stumbled upon was the area's preeminent authority on this condition and had more experience than anyone else in the area on the condition. E. B. had been led to this physician by the Holy Spirit.

A Physical Present from a Spiritual Solution

E. B. has now been on chemotherapy for one year. She was supposed to have undergone a biopsy that, according to the surgeon, might have left gaping holes on her face for life.

She opted for a spiritual, not a surgical solution instead. She prayed about what she could do. Convinced of a more conservative approach, she asked the surgeon to approach her condition conservatively (with a topical chemotherapy cream) rather than cutting off skin on her face.

Two years later, there is no evidence of cancer on E. B.'s face and no evidence that it has spread elsewhere. The physicians say the condition has disappeared and is unlikely to recur.

Since this incident, E. B. has celebrated fifteen years in business as a Christian businesswoman and currently employs five to six people. Her life is a testimony to the accomplishment of God's promise to whomsoever believes.

Life lesson 82: Until you laugh last, the Devil has no right to laugh.

You cannot be averse to war when you have an inner adversary.

Chapter Eighty-Three

Five Long Years

You shall serve the Lᴏʀᴅ your God, and He shall bless thy bread,
and thy water and take sickness away from the midst of thee (and)
nothing shall cast their young, or be barren in thy land.
—Exodus 23:25–26

S. T. (not her real name) was forlorn. She had a daughter, but she wanted another child. She and her husband were unable to conceive, however.

She poured out her heart in my clinic, and we prayed for her and her husband at our Holy Ghost Night prayer meetings. In the next few months, I saw her at my church consistently.

She came with her daughter to midweek and Sunday services seeking an answer. Her husband was not yet comfortable with this new church, and as a result, there was a strain on their relationship. However, she learned to be patient and to walk in faith and trust God for her miracle.

It's a Boy!

About three months later, she discovered she was pregnant. It was a miracle. She had not done any assisted reproductive techniques (ART) or gynecological procedures, but she was pregnant!

Her husband, seeing what God had done, started coming to church more regularly. He came to me and thanked my family and me for our assistance.

At the end of a trouble-free pregnancy, she delivered a bouncing baby boy. She is evidence of the gospel to the nations of the earth that truly "children are an heritage of the Lᴏʀᴅ and the fruit of the womb is his reward" (Psalm 127:3).

Life lesson 83: What Goes does in one area, He will do in all if given the opportunity.

Intimidation is a result of timidity, discouragement is due to lack of courage, feelings of inferiority come from living in fear, and insecurity comes from a lack of security in God.

Chapter Eighty-Four

Set Free from the Spirit of Suicide

The thief cometh not, but for to steal, and to kill, and to destroy: I [Jesus] am come that they might have life, and that they might have it more abundantly.
—Romans 10:10

T. H. (not her real name) appeared to have her mind elsewhere. She and her husband had just joined my church. While he was excited with church, she always looked forlorn and overwhelmed with life.

On their next visit to the church, I introduced myself to them. Over time, I met their three lovely children and their extended family. My wife and I even became godparents to their seven-year-old daughter.

There was, however, a dark secret T. H. was keeping to herself. She had been diagnosed with major depressive disorder (MDD) and had stopped taking her medications when she lost her medical insurance. She was facing recurrent relapses in mood and lived in a state of melancholia. She was having suicidal thoughts again, and she knew she needed urgent help.

257

I Do Not Want to Live Again!

T. H. accosted me at church and said she needed to talk to me. I could see the pain in her eyes and the sadness in her countenance. I prepared myself for something unsavory.

She wanted help immediately because the day before, she had attempted to kill herself by slashing her wrists. She had been rushed to the hospital. Her wrist was sutured, but she still felt suicidal. I prayed for her, cast every demonic spirit of suicide out of her, and asked her to read my book *Fear No Evil*.

Two weeks later, before the whole church, T. H. testified that she had been delivered from the spirit of suicide and depression.

She said she felt happier than she had ever been even though she had not started any new medications. Her countenance was brighter, a spring was in her step, and a smile had begun to emerge at the corners of her mouth. The Jesus who gives abundant life was working His life in her!

Life lesson 84: Suicide is not a side effect of mental disease but a demonic spirit.

God is a finisher who never abandons a project.

Chapter Eighty-Five

Multiple Sclerosis Mutilated

Trust in the LORD with all thine heart and lean not unto thine own understanding. In all thy ways acknowledge him, and he shall direct thy paths. Be not wise in thine own eyes: fear the LORD, and depart from evil. It shall be health to thy navel, and marrow to thy bones.
—Proverbs 3:5–8

H. D. (not her real name) had always had first-class vision, but she suddenly began to experience fogginess and some blindness in her left eye. As a mother of four, a busy housewife, and a final-year student of surgical technology, she didn't think much of it.

A month and a half later, the deterioration in her vision had become so marked that she was literally going blind. She saw an ophthalmologist who advised her to undergo magnetic resonance imaging (MRI) of her spine and brain.

The MRI results were suggestive of multiple sclerosis (MS). Doctors advised her to undergo cortisone treatments and chemotherapy, but those treatments had little to offer in the long term. That was when H. D. turned to God for a miracle.

I Curse Blindness

Assisted by her husband and children, H. D. walked up to the front of the church. This woman of God who had prayed for many hundreds needed a miracle of her own.

As led by the Spirit of God, I stretched out my hand and started praying for her. In that prayer, I cursed blindness and cast out MS. We called forth perfection on her body and declared it so.

She returned in a few weeks and declared to the whole church that she had been healed of impending blindness. After the prayer, she had noticed improvement in her vision, and the neurologist declared her MS-free.

She finished her degree and currently works at an eye doctor's office! As a beneficiary of supernatural eyes, she wants others to be blessed with natural eyesight. Praise God!

Life lesson 85: Faith is the currency of heaven, and no transactions occur in the kingdom of God without it.

*If your Bible is torn apart,
your life will not be.*

Chapter Eighty-Six

Determination against Termination

Lo, children are an heritage of the LORD: and the fruit of the womb is his reward.
—Psalm 127:3

R. D. (not her real name) is a renowned gospel singer in the United States. At a recent gospel show, she discussed her birth and the controversy surrounding it.

In the mid-1970s, her mother was suffering from chronic headaches and vomiting. She was evaluated at a university hospital and underwent computer tomography (CT) scans on her brain as well as other tests.

A few weeks after, however, the medical team discovered she was pregnant. Considering the radioactive rays from CT scans, the physicians counseled R. D.'s mother to terminate the pregnancy to save the fetus a lifetime of disability.

We Are Not Having That Discussion

R. D.'s mother was surprised to hear she was pregnant but she became even more alarmed when the physician suggested termination. A holy revulsion arose in her. She dismissed the recommendation from the medical team. She told them in uncertain terms that she was keeping that baby no matter what.

When they tried to convince her otherwise, she called her husband to come and get her. Again, she told the medical team she was not having an abortion.

Nine months later, R.D. was born beautiful and healthy. She has grown up to bless the world with her life-giving gospel music and is fast becoming Christian gospel's roving ambassador.

Her story was made possible because of one woman's determination to give life to an unborn child. One moment of determination can terminate a lifetime of capitulation if done in obedience to God's Word.

Life lesson 86: Determination is what makes you who God wants you to be.

God restores the family before He restores the church and the nation.

Chapter Eighty-Seven

Missing a Mother but Loving a Laborer

*I had fainted, unless I had believed to see the goodness
of the Lord in the land of the living.*
—Psalm 27:13

R. T. (not his real name) was estranged from his wife. Conflicts with his erstwhile wife and his children were continuing, and he moved into another relationship.

R. T.'s wife entered a new relationship as well and became pregnant by her new lover. At about six months of pregnancy, she was driving home from her lover's home with her four children by R. T. when the unexpected happened. A truck hit her car, and she and her unborn died. The four children survived.

From Trauma to Triumph

R. T.'s children were in shock, traumatized, when they moved back in with him. They couldn't believe they had just lost a mother and a sibling in one moment of madness.

In the years after the tragedy, R. T. tried to heal their wounds through labors of love, but they treated with him utter contempt. They complained about his attitude toward their mother while she was alive. With an escapist idea, they thought if he had been there, she would never have died.

In one of the overflow Sunday services at the Assembly, while R. T. was ministering in the choir, his teenage daughter ran on the stage and hugged him in a deep expression of love. He was soon surrounded by his other three children. Amidst loud wailing and expression of deep emotions, R. T. said, "This is a God thing."

This family healing stirred a well of spontaneous emotions in the congregation, and for another hour, different families came up to confess their schisms and conflicts and ask God for restoration.

Today, R. T. and his children (and his new wife and her biological children) are a happy and committed family at the Assembly West Monroe. The children are excelling in school, and R. T. is rising in his career as a foreman. Labors of love, according to Hebrews 6:10, will never be forgotten and always be rewarded.

Life lesson 87: Love is a seed that always yields fruit; if not now, it will in the future.

It is frustrating trying to become who you already are in Christ.

Chapter Eighty-Eight

I Can Hear Again!

"(They) were beyond measure astonished, saying, He hath done all things well: He maketh both the deaf to hear, and the dumb to speak" (Mark 7:37).

R. B. (not her real name) had suffered severe strep throat a few years after being born. Informed by her physicians that she would never hear again (as her hearing had been irreversibly damaged by the bacteria), she struggled through school impaired by both physical and psychological constraints.

To remedy the process, she underwent eight surgical procedures, including a cochlear implant and several tympanostomy tube placements without success.

At age sixteen, while attending a regular Sunday evening service at the Assembly West Monroe, she noticed she could hear perfectly in her right ear. She was so astounded at this newly improved hearing ability that she ran to the pulpit screaming, "I can hear again!"

Hearing, Holy, and Whole

After her healing, R. B. went from being an average scholar to a dean's list student. She received a national award that sent her to one of the best Christian colleges in the country on a six-year scholarship. She's now in a postgraduate program designed for those with bachelor's degrees seeking to earn higher degrees. She is in the topmost group academically at her school.

The turnaround in R. B.'s hearing remains a milestone in her life. She has set her eyes on reaching spiritual heights in the kingdom, and she is accomplishing that by hearing and obeying God's Word unequivocally.

She maintains purity in her walk with God; her relationships have been exclusively with those who exhibit stellar Christian qualities. As she said, "I don't want to be the spiritual leader in my own home when my husband is there."

Life lesson 88: Resting in God is synonymous with deliverance, but rebelling brings destruction.

It is not over until God says so,
and by then we will have won.

Chapter Eighty-Nine

Rescued, Restored, and Revived

I will restore to you the years that the locust hath eaten, the cankerworm, and the caterpiller, and the palmerworm, my great army which I sent among you. And ye shall eat in plenty, and be satisfied, and praise the name of the LORD your God, that hath dealt wondrously with you: and my people shall never be ashamed.
—Joel 2:25–26

F.U. (not her real name) endured deprivation, demonic oppression, and disease for more than ten years. She started using drugs at age twelve, and that snowballed into an alternative lifestyle and unethical notoriety.

She had a child out of wedlock at age twenty-two whom she gave up for adoption because of her complicity in drugs and crime. She spent time in six different drug rehabilitation facilities without any improvement. In 1994, she checked into Teen Challenge New York as a last resort.

In less than a month of following the Teen Challenge guidelines for drug rehabilitation, she had no withdrawal symptoms or drug cravings. She had been set free by the power of God from drug addiction, an alternative lifestyle, and a life of sin.

Complete in Him

After spending two years at Teen Challenge, New York, F. U. returned to West Monroe, Louisiana. She enrolled in Bible school and married a fellow Bible school student.

While married, her husband physically and mentally abused her. She sought counseling, but when her husband refused to change, she asked for and got a divorce.

In the meantime, however, she had become pregnant. During the pregnancy, doctors told she had cervical cancer and would suffer complications from it for life, and she was only thirty-six.

She received chemotherapy and radiation therapy after the pregnancy. The consensus from the medical experts was that she was beyond surgical intervention and should prepare for the worst.

Five years later, F. U. is a graduate of the School of Urban Missions (SUM) Bible school, lives in West Monroe with her daughter, and is enjoying life to the fullest. She is planning to open a women/children's rehabilitation home for women on drugs.

There have been no additional signs of cervical cancer, and her doctors tell her she is nothing less than a miracle. She is complete in Him—Jesus—after twenty years of looking for completeness in sex, substances of abuse, and sin.

Life lesson 89: If you get satisfied with anything or anyone else, it is an empty hope that won't last.

If it can be fired by the Holy Ghost, it must not have died.

Chapter Ninety

The Woman Who Walked Upright

I am the Lord *your God, which brought you forth out of the land
of Egypt, that ye should not be their bondmen; and I have broken
the bands of your yoke, and made you go upright.*
—Leviticus 26:14

Betty Baxter was brought up in a Christian home in Minneapolis,
Minnesota. Ever since she was a child, she had known nothing
but pain. She suffered from severe scoliosis that had crippled
her to the point of incapacitation.

After giving her life to Jesus, she understood that the will of God
was to heal, not hurt; to deliver, not destroy. Without bitterness,
grudges, or envy, she waited devotedly for God's healing stream.

One day, while in a coma, Jesus appeared to her and told her He
would heal her on the first day of autumn at 3:00 p.m. She asked her
mother to buy her a blue dress and white shoes for the occasion. Her
mother told her God had given her the same date and time for her
healing. Their expectation was pumped, and they waited earnestly.

Happy, Holy, and Healthy

The day Jesus healed her, Betty stood up straight, and for the first
time, stood taller than her three-year-old brother. There was no scar

or surgical incision. In less than a second, she was straightened by the power of God.

Betty's parents, siblings, and neighbors witnessed the miracle. The local newspaper reported her story. Betty went on to become a healing evangelist alongside Oral Roberts, sharing her testimony at his crusades.

Betty Baxter's story has brought thousands if not millions to the cross of Jesus Christ and reawakened the power of devotion in capturing Jesus' attention.

Life lesson 90: Give God your mess, and He will turn it into a message.

Faith believes God "will,"
not just He "can."

Chapter Ninety-One

As Old as Sarah

I have made thee a father of many nations, before him whom
he believed, even God, who quickeneth the dead, and calleth
those things which be not as though they were.
—Romans 4:17

R. M. (not her real name) was forty-four and still unmarried. She had waited for God's choice, but her hopes for a husband were beginning to fade. However, the fact she was an ardent worshipper of God and a faithful member of her congregation kept her hopes alive.

When she was forty-five, God sent her a husband who was a believer and committed to doing things God's way. After a brief time of courtship, they tied the knot and earnestly waited to start a God-centered family.

For six years they waited for God's promised seed. R. M. was on several occasions teased as being as "old as Sarah" and therefore not a viable candidate for carrying a pregnancy.

In spite of all the naysayers and biological odds against her, R. M. held on for God's promised child. She believed God, and she had a testimony.

Believable, Doable, and Sustainable

At age forty-nine, R. M. discovered she was pregnant. She and her husband were ecstatic with joy, but her medical providers were apprehensive. They told her the baby would be deformed or the birth premature, but she stood her ground.

She knew since God had allowed her pregnancy, He would bring it to fruition. She refused to abort the baby but confessed God's words over herself daily. Her medical providers warned her on the dangers of a fifty-year-old having a baby for the first time, but she reminded them of Sarah and Abraham, who were ninety and a hundred respectively when they had their first baby.

R. M.'s baby came full term and was perfect on delivery. He is currently starting elementary school. R. M. and her husband are blossoming in marriage and ministry. As a result of their being witnesses to the faithfulness of God, they want to help others stand in difficult times for their timely promise.

Life lesson 91: God is never a moment late or a minute early.

Start by doing what is necessary, then do what is possible, and suddenly you are doing the impossible.
—Saint Francis of Assisi (1182–1226)

Chapter Ninety-Two

Overcoming Myelomenigocele

And His name through faith in his name hath made this man
strong, whom ye see and know: yea, the faith which is by him hath
given him this perfect soundness in the presence of you all.
—Acts 3:16

S. R. (not her real name) was born with spina bifida, a major defect of the spinal cord that causes it to literally stick out of the skin.

Because of S. R.'s spinal protrusion, she developed weakness in both legs. She underwent spinal surgery three hours after her birth; physicians told her family that as a result of the surgery, she might never walk if she even survived the surgery.

S. R.'s Christian parents and grandparents, however, believed in the power of prayer. Her grandparents attend the Assembly West Monroe and sought God's face for a favorable surgical outcome.

In His Hands

S. R. successfully survived the procedure, but she was left with a limp in her step. Her classmates later teased her for her awkward gait, and as a result, she left high school in tenth grade.

She received a Graduate Education Diploma (GED) through home schooling and enrolled in a one-year Bible school (Master's commission) and graduated with a Bible school diploma.

In spite of all the odds she has faced in life, S.R. is doggedly and successfully pursuing her future. She currently works with disabled children even though she is disabled herself. She serves as an inspiration to other people, and her courage and determination are evidence of a life healed of disability.

Life lesson 92: To reign and train others is our mandate.

Your miracle is either coming toward you or going past you every day.

Chapter Ninety-Three

God—The Healer of Marriages

Thy Maker is thine husband... for the LORD hath called thee as a woman forsaken and grieved in spirit, and a wife of youth, when thou wast refused, saith thy God. For a small moment have I forsaken thee; but with great mercies will I gather thee.
—Isaiah 54:5–6

On a midweek service, God spoke to me about E. M. (not his real name) who was sitting in front of me. At that time, we had been asked to pray for our neighbors. After having prayed for him, I gave him the word God told me to give him.

I told him God said He was going to heal his marriage. He was sitting with a male friend of his, but he immediately broke down and started rejoicing. He said that he had been praying for his marriage and that this word was a confirmation of God's righting the wrongs in it.

E. M. had a blended family. He had previously been married and went into his current relationship with four children. E. M.'s second wife had three children. He was having difficulty disciplining his wife's children, and this was causing friction in his marriage.

Reversal of Hate and Revival of Healing

E. M. started coming with his formerly estranged stepchildren to subsequent services. They were participating in children's church and loving every minute of it.

The hatred E. M.'s children had for him dissipated. In its place came love, trust, and honor. Instead of spending Wednesday and Sunday nights in front of the television and with video games, they ardently attended church.

The remarkable experience the family had and has now in church caused a healing of the sour relationship between E. M. and his wife. They are living in more love today than they had ever before because the God who heals bodies can also heal marriages.

Life lesson 93: One word from God can change everything.

What men call opposition,
God calls opportunity.

Chapter Ninety-Four

Healed in Heart and Full of Faith

He shall not be afraid of evil tidings: his heart is fixed, trusting in the Lord.
—Psalm 112:7

B. W. (not his real name) is a legendary singer and pastor at my church. Currently in his seventies, he and his amiable wife have held out the torch of the gospel for decades without wavering.

B. W. started having heart problems in the last few years. His doctors told him that he had atrial fibrillation. He became unable to sleep because of his rapid heartbeat.

While that malady was continuing, doctors also diagnosed him with diabetes, hypertension, and obstructive sleep apnea. He had been healthy all his life, so this sudden decline in health was not what he had expected.

Worst of all, though, was the fact that his health was deteriorating while he was taking medications supposed to treat the disease. That was when he knew medications were not the answer, and he turned to God for a miracle.

A Heart Fix

In a midweek service at the Assembly West Monroe, I preached about full faith and obtaining the miraculous from God. Afterward, I gave an altar call for those God said He wanted to do a heart fix on, and B. W. walked up. He received by faith the healing power of God, and as events unfolded, his miracle manifested.

He was unknowingly taking a medication for diabetes that was worsening his heart condition. That medication was being imported from Canada and was once seized at the border. Without the medicine, B. W. noticed he felt and slept better.

His wife investigated and learned that the diabetic drug that had been given to him by his physician was actually more detrimental than beneficial to his health. His heart was fixed by stopping that "poisonous" pill. He stopped it, and is hale and hearty today.

Life lesson 94: A heart fix is not a physical but a spiritual surgery.

When the immoveable meets the unstoppable, the lesser power must bow.

Chapter Ninety-Five

Devils Departed as
Jesus Joined Me

Know ye not that he which is joined to an harlot is one body? for two, saith
he, shall be one flesh. He that is joined unto the Lord is one spirit.
—1 Corinthians 6:16–17

U. M. (not his real name) is an accomplished builder and
painter. He is happily married and has built a reputation of
raising a well-esteemed family in the community. He saw
me as a patient and related his story from bondage to blessing to me.

As a young man, U. M. had lived a riotous life. He slept with harlots,
used drugs, indulged in alcohol, and practiced other vices. On one
binge occasion, he was arrested and incarcerated for illegal possession
and trafficking of hard drugs.

While in the jail, he cried to Jesus for help, and God answered him.
Through the Spirit, he saw devils coming out of his body. As he shouted
the name of Jesus, more devils came out. He cried out in his cell for
deliverance, and God answered him with fire.

No Turning Back

In ten seconds, U. M. was delivered from the strongholds of sex,
spiritual manipulation, and substance abuse. He arose from the floor
limp and weak but free of the devils he had seen coming out of his

body. Only the sweet smell of the Holy Spirit remained in his cell. He became a powerful vessel for God in that prison and gave testimony to the power of God to deliver.

On discharge from prison, U. M. maintained his Christian testimony. Even though he did not go through professional counseling or follow up on discharge with a rehabilitation center, he has remained a light to the world of Jesus' power to save.

Twenty-five years later, U. M. is still walking in divine freedom. He has not had a relapse and is prospering in health, marriage, business, family, and most important, in his Christian faith. He attends the Assembly West Monroe and has remained an invaluable resource to help mentor young men battling sin, sex, and substance abuse.

Life lesson 95: God wants our relationship, not their religion.

Life by logic is a life limited.

Chapter Ninety-Six

Raised Up out of a Sickbed

The Lord will strengthen him upon the bed of languishing: thou
wilt make all his bed in his sickness. I said, Lord, be merciful
unto me: heal my soul; for I have sinned against thee.
—Psalm 41:4

On a Sunday morning, God clearly told me He wanted to heal someone named Minnie who was sick and raise her up. The word went forth, but for three months, nobody named Minnie came forward. Three months later, however, the word was confirmed.

According to Mark 16:20, God "works... with his disciples and confirms the word with signs following." God had given the word and confirmed it with signs and wonders.

Heart Attack Repaired Supernaturally

"Minnie" was looking vivacious and full of vitality. Even at age eighty, she looked almost as young as her two daughters. She was in an ebullient mood as she recalled what had happened three months ago in church.

Her daughters were in the church service when the word of prophesy went forth. Unbeknownst to them, their mother was having a heart attack about that time.

On admittance to the hospital, the doctors evaluated her and did a workup for cardiac disease, but they could find nothing wrong with her heart. They told her, after a plethora of tests, that her heart was fully recovered and needed no further intervention.

She has returned to full-scale church activities and is full of faith and the joy of the Lord. She shares the testimony of her supernatural healing everywhere she goes. She is confident that since God could find her in her sickbed, he could heal anyone else who desires His ability.

Life lesson 96: Tests, trials, and tribulations are not enough to stop you from getting to where God wants to take you—a place of triumph.

God said it, I believe it,
and that settles it.

Chapter Ninety-Seven

Cerebral Malaria Cured
Miraculously

Heal me, O LORD, and I shall be healed; save me, and
I shall be saved: for thou art my praise.
—Jeremiah 17:14

T. M. (not his real name) is the thirteen-year-old grandson of
missionaries in Kenya. While on a visit to the mission field in
2011, he contracted cerebral malaria and became unconscious.
The family took him to a tertiary health center in Nairobi, Kenya,
where physicians gave him a slim chance of recovery. If he did recover,
thy were afraid he would have a loss of mental and neurological
faculties.

As one of the churches supporting their work in Kenya, our church
received word of this child's condition. They urged us to pray. My wife
and I led prayers for him in our cell groups and believed we received
assurance of his healing by faith.

The prognosis was grim—malaria kills more than a million
children a year in Africa. Cerebral malaria, which is the most severe
form of malaria, has a fatality rate of nearly 50 percent and leaves
more than 90 percent of its victims impaired neurologically.

We knew, however, God is greater than cerebral malaria!

The Power of Prayer

Prayers went up for T. M., and within three days, he regained consciousness. The hospital discharged him, and he reunited with his family in the United States.

He is in high school and has no neurological deficits or intellectual impairments. He is serving God in his local assembly and looks forward to returning to Kenya for more missions work.

All these things happened because someone somewhere understood the power of prayer. As Saint Augustine said while espousing the power of prayer, "Without us, God won't, and without God, we can't."

Life lesson 97: Prayer without faith is like a car without gasoline. It is going nowhere.

When you are kept by the power of God, you become untouchable.

Chapter Ninety-Eight

Eliminating Edward's Syndrome

The law of the Spirit of life in Christ Jesus hath made
me free from the law of sin and death.
—Romans 8:2

Drs. Chuka and Ndidi Anude are the proud parents of triplets, Jide, Meto, and Kene. They were born in 2010 after an uneventful delivery.

Before the delivery though, the perinatologist told them to consider terminating one of the triplets because it had sonographic and laboratory tests consistent with Edward's syndrome.

Edward's syndrome, otherwise called Trisomy 18, is a genetic disorder that is incompatible with functional life. More than 90 percent of those with this condition die in utero due to their multiple congenital anomalies including mental retardation, congenital heart defects, and microcephaly (small head, jaw, and mouth).

Standing Strong in the Storms of Life

Drs. Chuka and Ndidi Anude are medical doctors with a public health background, and they knew the gravity of the specialist's opinion. They were, however, Christians before they were clinicians, and they were believers before they were brilliant scientists.

They therefore rejected the claims of science and believed God's Word instead. They called their children blessed, not diseased, and candidates "for signs and wonders" (Isaiah 8:18).

Nine months later, their children were born without a defect. The medical personnel were amazed that, notwithstanding their findings, the child alleged to have Edward's syndrome came out intact, perfect, and complete.

Today, that boy is three and is intellectually, socially, physically, and spiritually sound. He is in the top tier for his age group, and his healing life testifies to God's power to heal, save, and deliver to the utmost.

Life lesson 98: In the light of God's Word, darkness has no power.

If I ever met a real Christian, I would have become one.
—Mahatma Gandhi (1869–1948)

Chapter Ninety-Nine

Blind but Beautiful

Thou shalt forget the shame of thy youth, and shalt not remember the reproach
of thy widowhood any more for thy Maker is thine husband (and) the L<small>ORD</small>
of hosts is his name... For the L<small>ORD</small> *hath called thee as a woman forsaken and*
grieved in spirit, and a wife of youth, when thou wast refused, saith thy God.
—Isaiah 54:4–6

Ms. A. T. (not her real name) passed away in 2011. She was
blind physically, but she was beautiful spiritually because
she refused the ugliness of unforgiveness and the scars of
betrayal.

Mrs. A. T. had been married to the love of her life and was doing
what she loved most—preaching the gospel. She and her husband were
serving as missionaries to the Native American population and had a
rapidly growing family of four children.

In the course of time, Mrs. A. T.'s husband began to have an affair
with their Native American interpreter. He eventually abandoned his
wife and children and ran off with this strange woman.

Mrs. A. T. was crushed, but she overcame bitterness and resentment
by holding onto the Word of God. Her health later suffered, and she
became blind as a result. She had to move into an assisted-living
facility, but she never stopped to complain or bemoan her situation.

The Greatest Christian I Ever Knew

Mrs. A. T.'s children were livid about their dad's attitude toward their mom. Their dad had brought all this on their mother and showed no sign of remorse or rapprochement. However, when they would lift up their voices to speak invectives against him, Mrs. A. T. would tell them not to say any ugly words about their father.

Her physicians marveled at her unlimited bundle of joy and excitement in spite of her constraints physically, socially, and financially. Her community knew her as a spiritual solution center who always wanted to pray for or help the needy in their times of trouble, and her children knew her as the praying mother who covered them with so much prayer that they are all serving God actively today.

Even though she was blind and abandoned as a young wife, the life of God in Mrs. A. T. resonated to those in her community. At her death, thousands came to pay their respects, including her physician. A Hindu by religion, he said, "Mrs. A. T. was the greatest Christian I have ever seen."

Mrs. A. T. was blind but beautiful because she showed the world Jesus. Her testimony included the specific comment by her son that that throughout her life he could not remember her speaking an evil word about anyone. Mrs. A. T. still lives on in her deeds and in her children, one of which is today a missionary to the same Native American tribes to whom she ministered.

Life lesson 99: Vengeance is the Lord's, and He will repay, not you.

God answers prayers in more ways than we can humanly imagine.

Chapter One Hundred

Clear (Cell) Miracle

What shall we do to these men? for that indeed a notable miracle hath been done
by them is manifest to all them that dwell in Jerusalem; and we cannot deny it.
—Acts 4:16

D. R. (not his real name) was five when he was diagnosed with
kidney cancer. He had a football-sized mass on his left kidney,
and the cancer had spread to his brain and lungs.

Physicians operated on his left kidney and started him on
chemotherapy and radiotherapy. He was given a death sentence and
told by the medical experts that he had a life expectancy of less than
three months.

D. R.'s condition was considered the most aggressive of all. Cancer
of the kidney is extremely rare at his age. It has a five-year survival
rate of 50 percent and a high recurrence rate of 15 percent.

D. R. needed a miracle, and medicine had done what it could. He
needed a supernatural solution or his young life would be over. As a
believer in Jesus Christ, D. R. took the medical verdict to God in prayer,
and God surprised him!

Supernatural Healing

After one year of chemotherapy and radiation therapy (to the
kidneys, brain, and lungs), D. R. became stronger than the medical

experts had expected. He had lost all his hair and became emaciated during the treatment process, but he slowly regained his strength.

Today, seven years later, he is a middle school student with no impairments academically, socially, or physically. He is fully recovered, and on his semiannual follow-up visits, he still shocks the oncologists with his full recovery.

Even though he is only a teenager, D. R. has become a leader in the children's church. He is more spiritually sensitive to and desirous of God's presence than his fellow teenagers. His life is a healing life because he is proof of the power of Jesus' blood to alter the status quo.

Life lesson 100: You don't have to look to the stars when you can look to the one who made the stars.

PART VII

Conclusion

Healing is the bread of the children of God (Matthew 15:26), and we are all called to healing lives. Healing should not be an exception but the rule, because Jesus came, died, and rose from the dead to accomplish our healing.

Isaiah 53:5 says Jesus "was wounded for our transgressions, he was bruised for our iniquities: the chastisement of our peace was upon him; and with his stripes we are healed."

Your healing is not in the future but is already accomplished in the past by the death of Jesus. Matthew 8:17 says, "Himself [Jesus] took our infirmities, and bare our sicknesses."

If it has already been accomplished, all you need to do is accept, acknowledge, and avail yourself the truth of its finished work in your life.

Contacts

Faith and Power Ministries is dedicated to showing the power of God once again to this generation. It is dedicated to ushering in the last days' glory of God and, in the course of doing so, turning lives around for the kingdom of God.

Our email is tobemomah@yahoo.com, and we can be contacted via email or via our website, www.faithandpowerministries.org. We currently reside in West Monroe, Louisiana, and can be reached at PO Box 550, West Monroe, Louisiana, 71294 USA.

Other Books by Tobe Momah

A General and a Gentleman (biography of General Sam Momah). Spectrum Books, 2003.

Between the Systems, Soul, and Spirit of Man (a Christian doctor's view on sickness and its source). Xulon Press, 2007.

Building Lasting Relationships (a manual for the complete home). Xulon Press, 2006.

Metrobiology: A Study of Life in the City. First edition (a doctor's daily devotional). Xulon Press, 2008.

Pregnancy: Pitfalls, Pearls and Principles. Westbow Press, 2011.

Ultimate Harvest: Five F.A.C.T.S on Fruitfulness and How to Grow the American Church Again. Westbow Press, 2012.

From Edginess to Eagerness: Taking the Church Back to Willing Service. Westbow Press, 2012.

Fear No Evil... By Hating Evil. Westbow Press, 2013.

Fear No Evil... By Hating Evil (a daily devotional). Westbow Press, 2013.

STEPS to the Altar: Why a Chosen Generation Is Living Ashamed. Westbow Press, 2014.

Summary

Out of a mid-sized suburban city and church in West Monroe, Louisiana, come these true stories of healed lives. These stories are catalogued by physician, preacher, and published author Dr. Tobe Momah.

Healing Lives chronicles one hundred true stories of supernatural manifestations in the midst of sickness and various other situations that were eyewitnessed or verified personally by the author.

These accounts include physical, spiritual, emotional, financial, social, territorial, and marital problems. They recount the ability of God to change ignorant losers into triumphant overcomers by the power in the name of Jesus.

These testimonies will leave you energized, strengthened in your faith to stand for Jesus, and expectant for the supernatural in your daily life. Happy reading.